AMPLIFY YOUR INFLUENCE

AMPLIFY YOUR INFLUENCE

TRANSFORM HOW YOU COMMUNICATE AND LEAD

RENÉ RODRIGUEZ

WILEY

For general information on our other products and services or for technical support, please contact our Customer Care Department within the United States at (800) 762-2974, outside the United States at (317) 572-3993 or fax (317) 572-4002.

Wiley publishes in a variety of print and electronic formats and by print-on-demand. Some material included with standard print versions of this book may not be included in e-books or in print-on-demand. If this book refers to media such as a CD or DVD that is not included in the version you purchased, you may download this material at http://booksupport.wiley.com. For more information about Wiley products, visit www.wiley.com.

Library of Congress Cataloging-in-Publication Data is Available:

ISBN 9781119858683 (Hardback)
ISBN 9781119858768 (ePDF)
ISBN 9781119858751 (ePub)

Cover Image: © Jorge Castillo
Cover Design: Wiley

SKY10082101_081624

To Maddy.

Everyday. For the rest of my life.

Contents

Foreword

TECHNOLOGY HAS ADVANCED our society more than we could've ever imagined. Sadly, our wisdom and emotional intelligence haven't advanced at the same speed. *Amplify Your Influence* is the first book of its kind to finally take what we have learned through science and make it applicable and approachable to not only leaders but anyone who needs to influence behavior. This book could not have come at a better time.

Years ago, I began my career at a leading US university. In contrast to the typical business professor, I had already founded, managed, or actively participated in several businesses in addition to having the requisite academic credentials including a PhD in economics. I saw this professorship as a real opportunity to observe and get to know students, with the goal of attracting the best ones to work in those businesses. What I discovered surprised and disappointed me. While I found those students to be remarkably well educated on the functional aspects of business—the hard skills such as knowledge of accounting, finance, business law, and project management—they struggled in important social interactions, with the basic soft skills such as delegating, communication, emotional intelligence, and mentorship. I brought this to the attention of the MBA director, stating that if I were encountering these difficulties, so were the other companies who were hiring our graduates and that we should be including these skills in our curriculum. He looked at me somewhat confused and said, "You understand that we do axioms, theorems, formulas, and principles here, hard skills; we don't get into that 'training stuff.'" Almost in disbelief, I asked, "So you want me to stand in front of 200-plus MBA students and tell them what it takes to be a great leader knowing we are setting them up for failure?" To which he responded, "Yes, as long as they pay tuition." So I did the only logical thing: I quit and started my own business school.

According to the president of the AACSB at that time, the major accrediting association for business schools, it was one of the very first business schools created by a private person. We began immediately to address these missing elements in leadership that I had observed and experienced. We engaged cognitive scientists, social psychologists, anthropologists, evolutionary biologists, instructional psychologists, and neuroscientists. Motivated and excited by the potential we observed in neuroscience, we organized the first ever NeuroLeadership Summit at our campus here in Italy. (If you have the ability to create a business school, why not put it in a great location?) Shortly thereafter, we co-created the NeuroLeadership Institute, giving us access to some of the world's best neuroscientists. Among many discoveries and wonderful aha moments, we created a personal development program called LIFE. A dear friend and student of LIFE, Marcelo Montero, was leading Cargill's Salt business at the time; he told me about this consultant he was working with who was applying neuroscience to help his leadership team communicate more effectively through storytelling, congruent body language, and the science of influence. He referred him to our LIFE program, and that is where I met the barrel-chested, deep-voiced, statuesque person by the name of René Rodriguez.

He sat front row, taking every possible note, asking every question he could. I was quite surprised at how engaged he was. I was the teacher; René was the student.

René had had a powerful LIFE experience, and then we went our separate ways, connecting from time to time.

A few years later I got a call from Marcelo saying that he felt I should connect again with René because he was doing something new, which might fit in with the work and research we were doing on leadership. Shortly thereafter, René and I connected again immediately, and the ideas began to fly. He asked me an interesting question: Given my 40+ years of experience researching leadership best practices, what did I see as being the next big step in leadership development? This was a question we had been wrestling with for years, and at our program, we had come up with a definition of leadership as being a *"group, an influential relationship, and a shared goal."* Our program was meeting the needs of the "group" component in that definition, and company strategy dictated the shared goal in most cases. I told René that what I felt was missing was the "influential" component. We agreed it was a complex area, and like many important personal and professional development needs, it had many moving parts. René continued to ask a wide variety of thought-provoking questions.

Finally, my curiosity was satisfied when René told me he had something he wanted me to see, to experience, something he called Amplifii. He told me it was focused on the influence component that is missing in most leadership development programs. He told me it would transform how we communicate and interact with others in our many important social events. Among many other very interesting findings, he explained with an enthusiasm that only René possesses how he had effectively tied the persuasion models of Aristotle to relevant neuroscience research. He explained how he had linked together the importance of framing, a concept made famous in its financial applications by Nobel laureate Professor Daniel Kahneman, with brain "sequencing" to offer his students a truly comprehensible, practical guide to narrative-building and, thus, to improving their influence abilities.

Then we ventured into conversations around the narrative gaps in disparate and remote workforces and how they created new opportunities for leaders to leverage branding and social media in new ways. He persuaded me that personal branding was no longer just about sales and marketing efforts; it is now essential in leadership and other communications. He called it their "leadership brand," something we, too, had been studying from a difference perspective. We, the science community, had identified a problem; René has had a solution for close to 20 years! A solution based on the very science upon which we based our personal development system. We had learned the power of science in giving learners the confidence to take those important first few difficult steps that often inhibit personal development efforts. René's Amplifii could not have arrived at a more important moment for all of us.

In the 30 years since I left academia proper to start my own business school, things have changed significantly in our need for soft skill development tools. While technology has certainly made our lives better, those improvements have not been without significant side effects. Just 50 years ago, most of us died very close to where we were born. Rapid, unprecedented developments in transportation, communications, and digital technologies have slowly and steadily allowed us to willingly move apart from each other while simultaneously throwing us together, mixing cultures, integrating nationalities, and transforming our former local worlds into one world that is global in all important aspects. The days of living in the same community for a lifetime, going to the same schools, churches, grocery stores, and barber shops as our friends and neighbors, our parents and grandparents, our teachers and their teachers are over. As a consequence, we really don't know each other, but we still want to believe we do. Those common unspoken narrative gaps in our conversations that our brains could so easily and effectively fill in based on our shared local life experiences are now often wholly inappropriate and inapplicable in our new heterogeneous global living environment.

How are you and I experiencing this? That same technology making our lives better has also spawned such recent phenomena as working with difficult people, conflict management, difficult conversations, difficult confrontations, bullies in the workplace, change management, and a host of other ineffective social interactions. The requisite social interaction skills, which are essential human skills, have not developed like they did in our past local lives—through face-to-face conversations, storytelling, narrative building, through effective, interpersonal influence. We now need to learn how to create those narratives more than ever before. Since we cannot rely on a base of shared-in-common experiences, we need to tell each other, to ask each other, to learn how to build those narratives. And every day that passes in our new global environment, that need gets greater and greater.

In this new global environment, it is not at all surprising, then, that those so fortunate to go through René's Amplifii in person feel like they have been given a new lease on life, a renewed ability to connect in meaningful ways with family, friends, and colleagues, in addition to clients and customers. We are truly wired to be social, one of the very few positive lessons we have learned from COVID. For those of us who have not had the fortune of going through Amplifii in person, there is *this* wonderful, poignant book that guides and supports us through the process, to reunite us with those important social skills.

As to my personal experience, learning the Amplifii methodologies was a profound experience for me—and this time,

René was the teacher, and I was the student, a very attentive student. I am a scientist who spends far too much time on *logos*, the data, statistics, numbers, and other logical components of discovery, in attempts to be persuasive. René patiently taught me that I was failing myself because I was leaving out the *pathos*, the heart, the emotion, the reason why others would feel the need or desire to listen. Importantly, I observed and experienced that his message reached beyond influence to one empowering people to do good in the world. Sometimes I wonder if René disguises his true intentions of making this world a better place with the cloak of business so he can reach the highly influential people of the world. With a mother who was a former nun, I don't think that's a far stretch. If you ever get a chance to meet him in person, I think you'll agree that he is different, and his heart is in the right place.

One year ago, I would have written this foreword from my scientific view of the world, and you very likely would not have read this far into it. Amplifii did that for me; I share its cherished skills with others every day through my interactions and communications. Every student of mine, whether undergraduate, graduate, MBA, or executive, will be enjoying a copy of this book. René is the teacher; we are his students. And now, thanks to this book and the energy René has put into it in delivering his important message, you, too, can be one of his students.

—Dr. Al H Ringleb, JD, PhD
President and Founder, CIMBA Business
Programs Professor, University of Iowa
Co-Founder, Neuroleadership Institute

Introduction

We all have ideas to share with the world. Whether we do that successfully in business and in life depends on getting others not only to listen but also to act on what we say. That's the power of influence, the capacity to have an effect on an outcome and to positively influence change.

Have you ever shared a story, and no one listened? Told a joke, and no one laughed? Or pitched a product, and no one bought it? These are painful, all too common scenarios that can leave us feeling alone and insignificant because of our inability to influence the world around us.

The good news is it doesn't have to be that way. Influence is a science that can be learned. AMPLIFII™, my proven successful approach to influence, is your guide.

Whether it's a manager trying to inspire their team, a parent providing guidance to a child, or a salesperson working to close a deal, the goal is the same—to influence an action or decision. Leadership is about influence, so is marketing, teaching, managing, parenting, policing, and communicating. Basically every profession and worthy act of life requires some level of influence for us to find success.

This book uncovers the hidden drivers that shape our decisions and behaviors. In these pages, you will see how susceptible we are to the influence of others. You will learn how people make purchases and decisions subconsciously as a result of the stories others share and, how sequence—the order of things—matters more than substance.

Most people don't realize that the opportunity to influence is everywhere. Simply understanding that possibility can have an immediate impact on anyone's ability to communicate ideas more effectively. That's why learning to harness the power of influence—to AMPLIFII it—can transform our lives, increase our happiness, and help us find new levels of success.

Imagine the feeling of having people listen intently to your business proposals, laugh hysterically at your jokes, and be captivated by your ideas. That ability to capture attention gives us the opportunity to share ideas so they can be heard. That is the feeling of influence, the feeling of significance, and of having an impact on the world around us.

Wouldn't it be great to have the wisdom and skill set to truly influence others and better affect outcomes? Anyone can learn how to make that happen with the right tools and knowledge. AMPLIFII, my approach to applying the science of motivation, attention, storytelling, and body language, will show you not only how to recognize and create moments of influence but also how to leverage them to transform your personal and professional life.

Influence is the most powerful skill for success when we learn to use it properly and ethically. The ancient Greek philosopher Aristotle was the first to recognize this power of persuasion and how to harness it. I'll delve into the elements of what later became known as Aristotle's rhetorical triangle along with two other often forgotten motivational appeals and why his wise words from more than 2,000 years ago matter even more today in any discussion on the power of influence.

This is your playbook to maximize your personal and professional influence. It's a journey we will take together with the goal of learning how to become a better leader and influencer in all you do.

In these pages I'll introduce you to the simple AMPLIFII formula, and you'll join thousands of others who have learned what it takes to become a more powerful communicator, influencer, and leader. With AMPLIFII methodologies, you'll immediately realize the impact you have on others when you communicate authentically and effectively. As a leader you will be better able to share your vision, gain buy-in from your teams, and present difficult information in a way that keeps others engaged and drives action.

You'll also learn to better understand and use the power of storytelling. Some of the most influential leaders—from Nelson Mandela to Winston Churchill, Jim Rohn, and Steve Jobs—weren't just great speakers. They were also master storytellers who could create pictures with carefully chosen words and deliver them powerfully.

Their stories alone, though, weren't what captivated listeners. It was how these leaders told their stories and their ability to incorporate their messages within the stories. In these pages we will unpack the details of how that happens and provide a simple process to follow so you, too, can find your voice and the influence you need to get your ideas not only communicated effectively but acted on as well.

AMPLIFII starts with recognizing that all of us have one thing in common—a brain. Influence is about understanding how our brains and those of our audience process information. When we understand that process, our work, life, and business become easier. So do communications and interpersonal relationships, branding, messaging, conflict resolution, selling, and basically anything that involves human beings with brains working together to achieve a common goal.

Over the past 27 years of applying the neuroscience and psychology of leadership, communication, change, selling, and influence, I've learned certain fundamental truths that apply across industries and life that I share in AMPLIFII. I also will help you lay the foundation to become more effective—with the help of your own stories—as a leader and powerful influencer in all you do. I'll show step by step how the hidden drivers of behaviors lead to desired (and undesired) results and how to tip the odds in your favor.

You will learn how to build a powerful message that can preempt tough and predictable questioning as well as how to better understand and convey your message—whatever that message might be. I'll address how self-awareness, emotion, and storytelling are the secret ingredients for creating influence. I'll also discuss the power of message delivery—the sequencing, the body language, and the importance of each along with how to connect emotionally with your audience—of one, ten, 100, or 1,000, and up.

More of what you'll learn in these pages includes:

- Increasing self-awareness and presence to promote value-based leadership.
- Connecting to your origin story (what makes you who you are), values, and wisdom in your heart to unleash the power of your most authentic voice. (To influence people, they need to know you care.)
- Understanding how to engage people's hearts and minds by effectively communicating using the AMPLIFII formula.
- Increasing self-confidence to lead and communicate more effectively every day.
- Gaining a personal edge that empowers you to continue to flourish and succeed.

■ Elevating your game as a decisive influencer and authentic leader by learning to allow your heart to speak in the sequence that a listener's brain understands.

By the end of your journey through these pages, you will have a checklist to help prepare for every presentation or influence opportunity. Best of all, the checklist will become part of who you are. You will automatically begin to ask yourself those questions, follow those sequences, and reap the benefits of powerfully communicating messages with new levels of impact.

This book also includes simple exercises to help you better understand the concepts. Each chapter has powerful takeaways—essential points—at the end of each chapter.

I urge you to engage with these helpful approaches as well and to take as many notes in the margins as possible. Use your highlighter, underline concepts, take pictures, or whatever you need to do to remember.

This book will give you the tools to harness the art and science of influence. So let's get started on the path to becoming a more influential leader in all you do. I am honored that you have chosen this book as your guide. I look forward to taking the journey with you.

—**René Rodriguez**

PART

I

The Concept

1

The Power of Influence

The AMPLIFII™ Formula = Frame/Message/Tie-Down

AMPLIFII CAN INFLUENCE your business and your life for the better. But to share its powerful message, we first must be persuaded to listen. That's the most crucial challenge in the world of influence—getting others to listen to what we say.

We live in a world where seemingly everyone competes for our attention. We're constantly bombarded with emails, text messages, social media, meetings, advertisements, movies, television, and more. With advertising alone, the average person sees an estimated 6,000 to 10,000 ads delivered via a variety of formats every day—almost double the number of more than a decade ago.[1]

The reality is that all these distractions clamor for our precious attention. So do you. You want an audience to listen to what you say because you also have an agenda to market, whether you're selling a product, teaching a class, sharing a vision, managing people, or simply talking with another person.

Control the Room

Not long ago I gave a keynote address to a group of sales and marketing professionals in Dallas, Texas. The biggest challenge was not what to talk about—I had a clear plan—but that my speech overlapped with 600 conference attendees eating lunch.

That meant 600 people clanking plates, forks, knives, and dozens of amazing staff darting around doing their jobs oblivious to a speaker trying to deliver a message.

Tough Gig

For those who have never had to conduct business or deliver a speech over lunch, it's one of the most difficult gigs possible. That is, unless you know how to control the room. At this event, however, the good news was that another speaker preceded me so the worst of the clanking and most of the eating would be over by the time I got on stage.

My predecessor, however, wasn't so lucky. He didn't start his presentation by walking through the audience to gain their attention or offer any other upfront attempt at connection. Instead, he walked onto the stage and began his talk. He delivered a passionate speech from the heart and with incredible messages. The problem was that his speech was marred by clanking dishes, silverware, and rude attendees speaking loudly as if the speaker weren't there. He was obviously flustered, and those paying attention could feel his pain.

Lesson one: Gain control of the room and capture the attention of your audience.

The Right Approach

Then it was my turn. It seemed like the clanking and chatter got even louder as I walked onto the stage, and I knew I had to act quickly to avoid the imminent disaster that awaited me. After the obligatory welcoming applause, I immediately asked everyone if they would please stand up. When everyone was standing, I began:

> *All of us here in this room have one thing in common. We all need to influence others with our ideas in a highly distracted world. Today I find myself standing on stage in front of 600 people eating lunch, clanking plates, and having side conversations. It's a situation not that different from one all of you face regularly when trying to convey to potential clients your value proposition over that of your competitors.*
>
> *So what do we do? First, we want to ensure that we present our value in the best possible scenario. For me to do that, I have to ask two things. First, let's thank our wonderful staff here today for their great work. If you still have a plate, please place it on the tray and take it outside so we can begin. You have a minute or so to do that while I ask the audience to do a short exercise.*

By now the audience and staff were a bit shocked by my blunt beginning. Yet, they understood that it was highly relevant. They also could relate to my challenge because they wanted to learn how to capture the attention of their audiences, too.

I then went on to share a short story about my mother, who used to be a nun, and then asked them to shake the hands of three different people, come back, and sit down. By the time the handshaking was over, the staff had cleared the plates and the room was silent.

We all took a minute to reflect on the profound difference in the room. It was a teaching moment for the audience. They had just experienced firsthand how someone who wants to influence an outcome or decision first must eliminate the distractions—external or internal. In this case, the distraction was the room dynamics.

To deliver our ideas or messages, whatever they are, we first must figure out how to present them in the best possible setting or situation. That means eliminating the distractions so that others will listen and act on what we say.

Powerful Force

Whether it's a salesperson trying to close a deal, a parent offering guidance, or a manager trying to motivate a team, the goal is the same—to influence behavior, thought, or an outcome. Leadership is about influence, and so is marketing, teaching, managing, selling, and communicating. Our buying behaviors and the relationships we build are often the result of external influences that we're not even aware exist. As much as we may not like it, even our opinions are often based on the influence of others and the stories they share with us.

The opportunity to influence is everywhere. Just knowing that has a positive impact on our ability to communicate more effectively.

Unfortunately, many people don't understand the extent of influence and miss opportunities to advance their careers, earn greater income, and make a bigger impact on the world around them. That's why learning to harness the power of influence—to AMPLIFII it—is a crucial tool to increase success and improve the quality of life for all of us.

Simple Definition

Imagine walking into a room and people immediately sit up and listen to what you have to say. Or holding a meeting and participants quickly grasp and adopt the changes you propose.

This is influence, the capacity to have an effect on an outcome. That sounds simple. But in reality influence is a complex science as well as an art that can be learned to improve our ability to communicate and connect with others to get results. With the wisdom and skill set to truly influence others—to change other people's minds—we can better control outcomes in business and in life.

Influence is the *how* of leadership. Influence should be at the center of a manager's professional development, too, because in a world where people have choices, it takes more than command, control, or a title to affect outcomes. Human beings don't respond well to being forced, obligated, or pushed into doing something. They respond best when they are inspired to do so.

Inspiration

Working with tens of thousands of people over the years, I've learned that inspiration happens when our future actions align with what we believe in—our values. We are paid to come to work, yet some people struggle to find motivation. The same people, though, will work hard to build a home for a family through Habitat for Humanity and feel motivated and fulfilled at the end of the day even though they haven't earned a dime.

From the point of view of science and the brain, this inspiration happens when our prefrontal lobe (the executive center of the brain) connects with our limbic system, which is the home of our values. Our inspiration comes from that connection between what we value and the actions we take. This is also where the power of storytelling figures into influence. Storytelling is a powerful way to stimulate that connection and trigger inspiration. Stories create narratives that evoke emotions we adopt as our own. Those emotions often are so real that an individual can't tell the difference between what is real and what is fictional. That's why we cry during or after a movie. These are actors playing a role, yet we still cry. That's powerful. We'll talk more about that later.

Great speakers captivate and inspire their audiences with their stories, deliver their messages, and influence outcomes. The world's most powerful communicators and leaders also recognize how behaviors drive results and how to modify or influence certain behaviors to drive different results.

You can learn to do that too, no matter your audience. But you have to put in the work. Learning to be an influential communicator is like a baseball player learning to hit a fast ball or a chef learning to craft the perfect soufflé. It takes time, discipline, and effort. But the outcome is worth it.

Most importantly, being an influential communicator requires a connection to something that businesses traditionally shun—basic human emotion. Emotion—your heart and what you believe in—is your greatest strength and power to influence because it is what drives our behaviors. Every good sales professional knows that purchasing decisions are made with emotion and defended with logic. That's such common knowledge that there's a danger it's ignored. But think about it; the reason people buy is based on the one thing business professionals don't like to discuss—emotion. We need to stop, recognize, and begin to master this powerful and essential part of human existence.

Clubs in the Bag

Learning how to use the power of influence properly and ethically is an introspective journey for the rest of your life that can yield dramatic and gratifying results. Influence tools will dominate your life toolbox.

Those of us who play golf know that there's a reason to carry an entire bag of clubs. A golf course continually presents unique challenges depending on location and the shot. Each club is designed specifically to address various challenges. Club choice also depends on the ability of the person using the club and whether they have learned how to use it effectively.

There's a heavy driver to hit the ball long and hopefully straight, a putter to finesse the greens, and a sand wedge to handle tough situations.

Influence skills and techniques are no different. Our voice, storytelling ability, body language, and sequencing (the order of things) are all clubs in the bag of tools at our disposal. Each serves a different purpose depending on the situation and the goal. And as in golf, each skill requires practice and dedication to master.

We can't successfully play a round of golf with only one club, and no leader can be successful with only one influence skill. Individuals with a driver personality need to develop other softer skills to enable them to connect with people who may not respond to the driver leadership style. For the quiet, internal thinker, necessary skills to learn include how to be more assertive; otherwise those great ideas will never take flight.

If someone were to ask you what is the best golf club to use, you wouldn't be able to answer that without knowing where you were on the course and what your objective was. The same is true in leadership and communication. AMPLIFII, my proven approach backed by science and tools to amplify your influence, has been the guide for thousands of leaders across the world.

You Matter

Influence also is about personal significance and purpose—the impact each of us has or doesn't have on others and the world around us. One of life's greatest experiences is to have an idea that people listen to and act on. When someone hears what we say, it's empowering, energizing, and gives us purpose because we are making an impact on the world around us.

The opposite of influence is when no one listens, no one acts, no one buys the product we're selling. We feel alone, powerless, and even invisible. It's a feeling of insignificance because we have no impact on the world around us. When no one listens to us, we can feel as if we were invisible and had no value. That sounds dramatic, and it is, but it's true.

A leader who doesn't influence behaviors and thoughts may have a title but isn't leading or influencing a business. People may pretend to listen because they have to, but they really don't hear and definitely aren't engaged or inspired to act.

Take Responsibility

Chances are some of the most frustrating times in our lives happened when we couldn't influence others to listen to an idea, sales pitch, direction, or need. I know that was the case in my own life until I decided to take ownership and recognize that the problem wasn't others, it was me.

Canadian businessman, investor, and television personality Robert Herjavec often shares some great advice with competitors on the US television show *Shark Tank*: "It's not my responsibility to listen. It's your responsibility to make me hear." That simple philosophical change can make a huge difference in your ability to embrace what it takes to be influential and add value. The opportunities to innovate and disrupt happen when we take ownership of and surrender to the reality that we must add value and that the marketplace determines the value. Excuses and entitlement don't get anyone anywhere in the world of influence.

We can't get rich by demand or pity. Our proposals won't get accepted because people want to give us a break. We are selected because we communicate value to the people making the decision.

However, if there's a political component to a scenario—perhaps internal or external business politics—that's different and calls for a different approach. If someone is "out to get" someone else, that calls for the three Ps—predict, preempt, and prevent—to set yourself up for a win. Whatever the situation, though, we must learn to take full responsibility.

I also have learned that if others aren't listening, instead of being discouraged, take the time to figure out why. We need to become students and use those encounters as learning experiences because they give us so many insights.

Pay Attention

When you meet or listen to someone you really like, don't simply say, "That was awesome," and walk away. Stop to analyze why you felt that way. Recount everything about how you met the person, how they presented themselves, and what it was that attracted you. What did they say? How did they say it? Did they smile or not? What stories did they share? What did they wear? Was there a certain smell involved? Yes, the latter matters, too.

Conversely, when you encounter a person you don't like, don't just avoid them. Be curious and ask yourself what about the experience made you dislike them. What did they say? How did they act? All the above questions apply, too, because the answers will help you recognize what works and what doesn't in your own life.

Each of those scenarios has a formula that led to an outcome. One led to a pleasant experience. The other led to a negative one. It's important to study both formulas. Learn the formula that attracted you so you can replicate it and make others feel as positive as you did. Learn the formula that repelled you so you can make sure to never engage in anything that makes someone feel as you felt.

This isn't about snap judgments of other people. This is a way to build self-awareness and enhance your emotional intelligence quotient (EQ). If you feel one way when someone acts a certain way, then most likely others will feel similarly if you act that way.

Life always offers insights and clues into these little formulas for success if we just look for and listen to them.

Emotional Quotient

The cover of *Time* magazine, October 2, 1995, read: "What's Your EQ? It's not your IQ. It's not even a number. But emotional intelligence may be the best predictor of success in life, redefining what it means to be smart."[2]

I'll never forget that my mother, a successful change management consultant and thought leader, received dozens of copies of this from her clients around the country, accompanied by the same comment: "Magaly! This is what you've been teaching us!"

The article discussed the groundbreaking book *Emotional Intelligence*, by Daniel Goleman. Goleman, wrote that EQ, or emotional intelligence—not IQ—is the predictor of success. The concept redefined what it means to be smart and explained why so many CEOs were C students.

Goleman expanded on the groundbreaking brain and behavioral research done by psychologists Peter Salovey and John Mayer, who together introduced the concept in 1990. They defined emotional intelligence as "the ability to monitor one's own and others' emotions, to discriminate among them, and to use the information to guide one's thinking and actions."[3]

More on that later.

The why.   The success of Goleman's book was in part due to the fact it explained why so many individuals with high IQs don't do well in life while others who typically have lesser IQs do surprisingly well. Let's take a deeper look at the factors that figure into emotional intelligence.

These factors, including self-awareness, self-discipline, and empathy, equate to a new way of looking at intelligence and success that may not be hard-wired at birth. This perspective offers hope that we can improve the quality of our lives. Even though someone's EQ is molded by childhood experiences, it can be nurtured and strengthened throughout our life thus affecting our health, personal relationships, and work.

Emotional intelligence is a cornerstone of influence, and self-awareness is at its center.

Try the exercise below.

- Think back to a person you met who you immediately liked and with whom you clicked.
  - o Describe in detail what happened and why. What was the formula? What did the person say? How did they treat you? What questions did they ask? Be as detailed as possible in your responses.
- Think back to a person you met who you immediately disliked.
  - o Describe in detail what happened and why. What was the formula? What did they say? How did they treat you? What questions did (or didn't) they ask? Be as detailed as possible.

This same exercise works with former managers and bosses, as well as romantic partners. The goal is to build awareness of what creates positive experiences and what doesn't so we can learn to replicate the good and avoid the bad.

Apply the Learning

Take a moment to think about a time when you didn't feel influential or when people didn't listen to you and how it felt. Jot down your thoughts.

- *Think about why no one listened. Was it what you said, how you delivered the message, your appearance, your credibility, all of the above, or something else?*
- *If there's a visual of the event—even a selfie—look at it objectively. Is there anything that stands out as to why no one listened to you?*
- *Why do you think no one listened?*
- *Pay attention to anything in the encounter that immediately turned you off. That's also how others feel when your message turns them off.*

Now take a moment to think about a time when you felt very influential and people listened to you and how it felt. Write down those thoughts, too.

- *Think about why people listened. Was it something you said, how you delivered the message, your appearance, your credibility, all of the above, or something else?*
- *If there is a visual of the event—even a selfie—look at it objectively. Is there anything that stands out about why people listened to you?*
- *Pay attention to anything in the encounter that you quickly embraced. That's also how others feel when they accept your message.*

Building that self-awareness is really about understanding emotional intelligence in its purest form. Emotional intelligence provides plenty of insights into the role self-awareness plays in business, in relationships, and how we interact with people.

Emotional competencies.   There are five emotional competencies or skills that make up and help us understand EQ, including:

- Awareness of our own emotions. When we're unaware of our own feelings, we can't possibly understand the feelings of others and experience empathy.
- Control of our own emotions and not surrendering to impulsive feelings or responses. When someone sends a negative email, for example, we control the desire to lash out.
- Ability to assess the feelings of others. One way to do that is to read cues and clues in body language.
- Ability to recognize the capabilities of ourselves and others.
- Ability to successfully adjust our behavior to better relate to others.[4]

The best part about understanding EQ is that the effects are almost immediate. All it takes is a few successes, and you're on your way. It's like a snowball rolling downhill. The farther it rolls, the bigger and stronger it becomes. Eventually understanding the concept will transform your life.

Learned Behavior

Anyone can learn to capture the attention of others and influence outcomes with the right tools and knowledge combined with the AMPLIFII formula. It's a three-part formula—frame (context), message (core idea), and tie-down (the meaning/action). You'll learn more about that formula in detail throughout this book.

Remember, AMPLIFII takes the science and psychology behind our behaviors and combines that with an acute understanding of self-awareness, emotions, storytelling, body language, and more to help each of us better deliver our ideas to others. The result is the ability to enhance our message delivery and connect with our audiences—whether that audience is one person or 5,000. And in the process, we influence outcomes and improve our lives.

The Brain Connection

My journey to understand what makes people listen began years ago when my mom asked me a simple question, "What's the one thing all of us have in common?" The answer (which I didn't get at the time): We all have a brain.

An Easier Life

As previously explained, when we understand how the brain works and why, life and business can become easier. So can communications, interpersonal relationships, branding, messaging, conflict resolution, selling, and basically anything that involves humans working together to achieve a common goal. The reason it becomes easier is that we are working with the sequence of the brain instead of against it.

Over the past 27 years of applying the neuroscience and psychology of how the brain works in leadership, communication, change, selling, and influence, I've learned certain fundamental truths that apply across industries and life.

For example, in unsuccessful attempts to communicate a message, we often skip over the formulation—how we arrived at the message—and jump straight to the logical conclusion. We lead with an answer before we ever lay out the challenge and why we need the solution.

In simple arithmetic 1plus 1 equals 2. It's easy to understand, and it works. But for the more complex, again using a math example, 2,000 divided by 72 equals 27.7777778. I didn't arrive at that number in my head; it required a sequence of steps, a formulation to figure the answer.

It's the same when we attempt to sell an idea, product, or service or try to convince an audience of the efficacy of a new approach. We have to step-by-step lay out the details and then deliver the message. Our brain needs that frame of reference. Framing is how we understand the structure of reality; frames are constructs of reality. (More about framing later.)

Selling Thoughts

One of the fundamental life skills is learning how to sell a difficult or different idea whether it involves someone working with you, liking you or your product or service, or even believing in you. We all do that to some extent every day consciously or subconsciously with our thoughts, emotions, actions, words, appearances, and presentations.

A salesperson trying to sell a product or service hopes to drive the behavior of a potential client. A parent with actions and words tries to influence a child to brush their teeth or act a certain way. One person wants a date with another, so they behave in a way to positively influence the decision. Even marketing pieces—online, in-person, and in the media—are composed and presented in specific ways designed to influence others to pay attention and listen to the message.

Resistance

Anytime we engage in goal setting or business or strategic planning, we typically look first at results. Behaviors drive results—positive or negative. So when we don't like the results, we look to change our behaviors.

That's not a new formula, but it's a misleading one because it fails to account for the reality that most people don't respond well to behavioral changes. They resist them. That's one reason why adoption of new technologies often is slow, why so many companies fail to execute on strategy, and why most New Year's resolutions are abandoned shortly after the new year.

Resistance is a part of the human experience. We need to accept that and become a master of why people resist change. When we understand the why, we can learn to influence the desired behavior.

The irony in resistance and the brain is that the No. 1 task of the brain is survival, and often the changes we try to make like eating better, exercising more, and reducing stress are necessary to ensure survival. Yet we still resist those changes.

For years, that frustrating reality has been my center of study to understand the brain. I've learned that it all comes down to stress. The brain uses stress as a measure of threat. If we're threatened by a bear in the woods or a shark in the water, obviously that triggers stress and specifically the release of cortisol in the brain. The chemical reaction that follows is designed to keep us alive in those situations. And it usually works, too. The challenge, though, is that many situations in life cause stress but won't kill us. Yet they still trigger the same chemical reaction.

Influence is about causing and affecting change and therefore is likely to create stress. So to be effective, we have to be well versed in understanding how stress works, what causes it, how we can cause it in others, and what causes it in us.

Is resistance a result of the message, the presentation, the emotion, the lack of connection, or some other external force? The answers to those questions can help us understand how to successfully influence change. As we become students of our own experiences, we can learn the right and the wrong ways to do things. More on stress later.

Powerful Takeaways

- Influence is not something that's learned overnight. It's an art that requires many skills and takes practice to master.
- Influence also is about personal significance and purpose—the impact each of us has or doesn't have on others and the world around us.
- The various influence skills and techniques each serve a different purpose and are tools in your life toolbox.
- Become a student of your own experiences. If you meet someone and like them, figure out why. It's the same if you don't like someone. You'll be surprised at how much your experiences can teach you.
- Emotional intelligence is a cornerstone of influence, and self-awareness is at its center.
- Too often we skip over how a message was formulated—the sequence of steps we went through to develop a message. Selling an idea, product, or service or convincing an audience of the efficacy of a new approach requires us to step-by-step lay out the details and then deliver the message.
- Our brains need a frame of reference to act. Framing is how we understand the structure of reality.
- Resistance is part of the human experience. We must learn to understand why people resist change and learn to influence a desired behavior.

2

The Hidden Drivers of Influence

"Centuries later Aristotle's teachings on persuasion and influence still ring true."

—René Rodriguez

MORE THAN 2,000 years ago the Greek philosopher Aristotle was the first to recognize the power of persuasion and its role in argumentative thought. He identified critical elements—what he referred to as emotional appeals—three of which became known as Aristotle's rhetorical triangle.

Those three critical elements include *logos* (logic), *pathos* (emotion), and *ethos* (credibility). You may have heard these words before, but in-depth understanding of them is crucial to the AMPLIFII formula. Mastery in these areas will propel you even further and garner bigger results.

Aristotle took his thoughts on persuasion further and included two additional, often overlooked appeals, *kairos* (timeliness), and *telos* (purpose). I believe the two latter appeals are even more important to influence and persuasion today.

Wisdom for the Ages

Aristotle's teachings ring true all these centuries later. Psychologists now refer to these elements as motivational appeals necessary for persuasion. Let's look more closely.

Ethos

Would you take advice on how to lose weight from someone who is overweight? What about how to make money from someone who is broke? Of course not, because they have no credibility. They lack ethos. Ethos is your credibility and character.

Another easy example of a person who lacks ethos is someone on social media with only a few followers trying to demonstrate how to increase your own social media following.

Ethos also is the essence of who you are and how you are known. It's critical to your personal brand. Basketball great Michael Jordan used his ethos to propel the Nike brand, and we saw what happened and continues to happen. Actors use their names and sometimes their faces to bring awareness to social issues.

Why we build ethos. Before I became a speaker, my sales cycle—the time it takes to close a deal from start to finish— was six months to a year or longer. Then, after my first big-stage speech, CEOs began to reach out to me. After the first magazine cover, the first telephone call wasn't to ask, "What do you want?" It had changed to, "What will it take to get you to come to our company?"

The game completely changed because my ethos had grown. When people ask what's the biggest and most immediate business benefit of becoming a speaker, my answer is simple. It shortens the sales cycle and increases the fees for your services by creating leverage and compressing time. Leverage happens when we have to say less and more happens. Compression of time happens when we move from one-on-one meetings to one on many. That can mean 100 meetings that are one-on-one, or one meeting with 100 people.

Social media connection. Having a great social media presence also creates ethos. Your number of followers has an impact on how people perceive you. It's not everything, but that vanity metric can boost your ethos.

More ethos builders. Other ways someone can grow their ethos include:

- Be the one in front of the room or on stage.
- Publish a book or article.
- Create a well-crafted introduction instead of a boring resumé; it sets the stage for your credibility.
- Get an endorsement or referral from a trusted third party.
- Have a professionally designed website with updated photos; optics matter.
- Develop a cohesive brand that creates confidence.
- Provide high-quality and memorable business cards; even in our digital age, any handouts should be high quality. Some people think business cards are outdated, but for those who want them, a quality card makes an impact.
- Pay attention to how you dress; like it or not, it matters.
- Develop a powerful voice. Hire a voice coach if necessary.
- Watch your personal hygiene; the perfect suit and well-crafted story can be immediately overshadowed by bad breath or body odor.

Ownership. Ethos is not something you own. We consistently see people make the mistake of thinking they own their ethos.

Instead, your audience owns your ethos; they grant you credibility. If you're a speaker at an event, your audience will give you ethos. But if you stand on the podium and are boring and provide lousy content, the audience will take back the ethos. Not only that, they most likely will tell others about your bad presentation, further harming your ethos.

You, the reader, have given me ethos by opening and reading this book. Without continued value in these pages, though, you will close the book forever. Ethos is a great accountability tool that keeps us all honest, myself included. It forces us to continue to create new content and stay focused. When we lose sight of that reality or become complacent, that's when we bomb on stage because our ego takes over. Those are the times we would like to forget. (I know that firsthand.)

We all know or have come in contact with speakers or leaders who think they own their ethos. We can feel their arrogance the moment they walk into the room. Unfortunately, today's fast-food, social media world supports some of those figures because they're entertaining. But let's go beyond the superficial to something deeper and more meaningful so we can learn to harness the power of true influence.

Speaking to an audience, running a meeting, or leading a group is a privilege. The audience or attendees have chosen to listen to you. The moment they grant you ethos is the moment you need to give it back. That giveback manifests as humility, gratitude, preparation, customization of message, connection with the audience, and even staying around afterward to shake hands and take questions.

Someone who is very successful and fails to give back ethos ends up with an overblown ego because they've lost sight of the privilege the audience has given them. The fact that they try to hold onto their ethos instead of giving it back creates a disconnect and is one of the fastest ways to lose influence.

Pathos

Pathos is the ability to reach someone else via a story, humor, or any appeal that moves that individual to connect emotionally. It's the ability to create empathy in others. Vulnerability is truly the superpower when it comes to pathos. Your ability to share your story, your struggle and not your success, is what matters.

A well-respected physician tells you to lose weight and eat better. He has the ethos; nonetheless, you brush him off with your response, "Thanks, doc. I'll start next week."

You shun the doctor's advice because he lacks pathos, the appeal to our emotions that drive our behaviors. No pathos, no behavioral change.

Connecting.   Often people communicate stories of success and triumph too quickly. That makes it difficult to connect with them. On the other hand, the story of struggle and failure is much easier to relate to. Imperfection is what makes us human, and someone who can't or won't tell that story has a hard time sparking passion in others.

When I speak—50 weeks a year—I invariably begin my speech with a story to connect with my audience before I deliver my message. If the audience is resistant, the story reflects a bit more vulnerability. We can't ask our audiences to do something we're not willing to do. (More on vulnerability later.)

Customers.   In today's highly competitive business environment, developing and managing relationships with customers or potential customers is a crucial differentiator. The emotional connection—pathos—is at the core of those relationships we build that lead to the person answering your telephone call, responding to your email, or truly listening to your offer.

Logos

Logos is the logical argument, the appeal to our sense of reason, the facts and figures. Aristotle in his day of mainly written or spoken words believed logos to be the most critical appeal in persuasion. Today with the dominance of social media, ethos and pathos tend to carry a stronger appeal. Of course, we still need logos/logic to buy into the message.

Imagine buying into the ethos of a presenter and the pathos of their story but having difficulty in understanding what they are asking you to do. You don't know how to act and are left with emotion without purpose; energy to act but no target—no logos.

In business, logos is critical and is what remains after pathos wears off. Without logos, we are left with buyer's remorse and cognitive dissonance. Logos is the plan, the steps, the agenda, the goals, the process, the rationale, the budget, the numbers, and the data.

Someone who has ethos and logos but no pathos lacks the emotional connection with others. With ethos and pathos, there's credibility and passion but no plan and no details to achieve the goal. And if someone has pathos and logos but no ethos, they lack the credibility to gain the followers to achieve the goal.

The Forgotten Two

Now let's take a closer look at Aristotle's "forgotten" emotional appeals that today are as essential to persuasion as those elements in the rhetorical triangle.

Kairos

Kairos translates from ancient Greek into "the right time" or timeliness. In the discussion of persuasion and rhetoric, kairos refers to relevance to the current era, or current zeitgeist. In other words, it's about taking advantage of the perfect moment to deliver a message and delivering it in a way that's relevant to those listening. The key word is *relevant*.

Word choice.   A training specialist was recounting a story about a plane accident to a group of young professionals. The audience listened intently until the older speaker began to talk about the *stewardess* who was bleeding and running up and down the aisle.

Suddenly, the speaker lost his connection to the audience. From that point on, it didn't matter what he said. No one listened because he had lost his relevance with those in the room, and all because he used outdated terminology.

Even though his pathos (emotion) was on point and ethos (credibility) was high, the speaker lost his audience because he was out of touch with kairos. He should have referred to the *flight attendant*, not the *stewardess*. Lacking kairos caused him to lose his ethos.

Kairos goes far beyond being politically correct; it's about being relevant and timely. Using kairos well means you tailor a message to your audience based on who they are and their current needs. It shows that you are current and in touch with the times versus out of touch and dated. You're also able to draw on current events while being sensitive to all sides of a story.

Kairos can make or break a business pitch. To raise capital, for example, if you are perceived as dated, not current, or too late to the game, you're done and out of luck.

Relevance.   Often, I'm booked months in advance for presentations and regularly check in with clients to make sure nothing has changed. The goal is to ensure the client's needs are the same and that my message is still aligned with their kairos. The last check-in sometimes is a few hours before the event and sometimes even less.

In one instance, a client approached me about five minutes before going on stage to tell me that their company had just been acquired and everyone was very frustrated with the situation. That's important information that affects my audience and my presentation. Knowing this, even a few minutes ahead of time, enabled me to make minor adjustments in my presentation to align with the audience's current reality. Because of that, we connected immediately, and the client was quiet satisfied.

Customization is a powerful influence tool, especially if you can pull from your immediate environment to make your story or message more powerful. At one event as I was being introduced and approached the stage, I passed a server delivering a plate with sizzling cheese to a customer. I took note of it and went on stage. Ninety seconds later I pointed out how we all live in a highly distracted world and need to capture attention "just like this gentleman's sizzling cheese on his plate. Our messages need a little more sizzle these days."

The man who received the cheese looked at me, nodded, and smiled. The audience laughed and leaned in more. I hadn't planned on using that frame as an example, but I was ready for it and it made sense.

Your audience.   Kairos sometimes can get confusing because an audience, demographics, or geography can change the relevancy of the message. For example, someone speaking to a group of young entrepreneurs referenced *The Partridge Family* to make a point. The audience, of course, had no clue the presenter was talking about a fictional TV family from the mid-1970s. Many of the audience weren't even born then.

Too often we overlook the importance of the audience in front of us, who they are, and their culture. Overlooking a culture happens frequently and with not so pleasant results. Coca-Cola is famous for its cultural blunders. When the company launched in China, apparently the company didn't think too much about kairos. The company chose the Mandarin translation of *Ke-Kou-Ke-La*. Unfortunately, in Mandarin that means "bite the wax tadpole" or "a female horse stuffed with wax."[1]

Another example I often share is that since I never knew my father, I used famous TV fathers as fictional role models. Some of my favorites include Uncle Phil from *The Fresh Prince of Bel Air*, Mr. Miyagi from *The Karate Kid*, and Dr. Huxtable from *The Cosby Show*. Those were great examples until Bill Cosby was convicted of horrible wrongdoings. I immediately stopped using Dr. Huxtable as an example. Continuing to use his name would have made me out of touch with kairos.

Kairos matters.

The good news is that youth today are great at reminding us how out of touch many of us are.

Telos

In Greek, the word *telos* means literally "the end." As it relates to understanding influence, telos is the end game, the purpose, the essential aim of a speech, a sales pitch, or a presentation. It's the point you hope to convey to your audience.

The telos of this book is to equip others with an understanding of the necessary skill sets to be a better influencer in their business and their lives. That's the same whether the goal is to become a better salesperson, better leader, better speaker, parent, friend, or whatever.

More about the Brain: The RAS

Making sense of all things that constantly bombard us is a job of the reticular activating system (RAS). It's a pencil-shaped part of the brainstem. Among other things, its job is to sift through all the clutter that constantly bombards us consciously and subconsciously and identify what is important—what's valuable—to each of us.

It's the filter that says, "Yes, listen," or "Forget it," and it's guided by our previous experiences, ideas, thoughts, feelings, and the power of influence.

The RAS enables us to filter out someone saying our name in a roomful of conversations. It enables us to pick out the conversation we want to hear or see the picture we want to see. To put the job of the RAS in perspective, think about all the sights, sounds, tastes, touches, moving objects, and more that are constantly present all around us. Better still, take a minute to stop and listen to all that you weren't paying attention to a minute ago. It's mind-boggling.

Part of the job of a communicator and an influencer is to manage that quest for attention. We have to learn to appeal to someone's RAS to gain their attention and to influence an outcome. Stories are one way to do that.

The RAS is also very sensitive to the stress response and can shut down our logical centers when under stress. Stress causes something known as "cortical inhibition" and is the reason that we do stupid things when we're stressed. At the same time, we can't function at our best because of this cortical inhibition.[2]

Managers versus Leaders

Too often people talk about how we need leaders not managers. In truth, we need both. Unfortunately, both can perform poorly.

The true art is knowing when to act as a manager and when to act as a leader, when to use authority and when to use influence, when to ask and when to tell, when to take over and when to let go. In every case, it is crucial for leaders and managers to understand the range of influence techniques they can use, know when and how to use them, build their power bases so they have the capacity to be influential, and sharpen their skills so they can influence people effectively.

AMPLIFII's methodologies marry the proven leadership best practices with what neuroscientists have discovered about the brain along with real-life applications with thousands of people.

Influence Is Leadership

Imagine a leader giving a great speech and earning a standing ovation or a leader running an amazing meeting with rave reviews. Now imagine that after the speech and meeting no one changed their behavior, no one did anything differently, and everything went back to exactly the way it was.

Would you say that the speech or meeting was a success? The bottom line is that leadership is about influencing behavioral change; therefore, there can be no leadership without influence. It is the *how* of leadership that requires leaders to have high-level skills in the art and science of influence.

Managers use influence, too, because only a fraction of managerial work can be accomplished through control and the use of authority.

The aim of both managers and leaders is to accomplish an organization's goals. Managers do it through plans, organization, processes, task assignments, measurements, and so on, but they must also direct people and manage their performance. It is impossible to manage people solely through command-and-control methods.

The Connection

People are human beings, not machines, mechanical parts, or assembly lines. They respond best when they are treated with the respect due human beings. People work best when they have a voice in how the work is done, and they remain loyal and engaged when they feel valued, trusted, well informed, and cared for. That's why the best managers also lead through the social and emotional approaches to influencing, not just the rational approaches.

Leaders lead by mobilizing people around a compelling vision of the future, by inspiring them to follow in the leader's footsteps. They show what's possible and motivate people to make those possibilities real. They energize and focus people on how to fulfill their dreams, give them a sense of purpose, and leave them with a profound sense of accomplishment when the work is done.

Leaders lead by modeling ways of thinking or acting and by encouraging new ways of looking at situations. By doing so, they give people the words and the courage to make those new ways their own. The best leaders are teachers, mentors, and role models—and they accomplish the majority of their work through influence, not authority.

In many cases, leaders and managers are one and the same. The division vice president, for example, who leads a team of people to accomplish what they might not have thought possible is also a manager. The manager who oversees a team's task performance but also looks after the team members' career planning and coaches them on developing their skills is also a leader.

Myths, Opposites, and Clichés

In these pages as we unpack the power of influence, there may be times when the AMPLIFII approach includes suggestions that are the opposite of traditionally accepted behavior. Or the approach may support an accepted "myth" or even use a tired cliché.

Just remember the golf bag analogy. Understanding influence and how to use it requires many different skills, each to meet different needs. The battle for influence isn't black-and-white. It isn't an either/or conversation. It is both, and it's nuanced like a particular golf shot and requires study, expertise, finesse, and the right delivery. If you don't make the shot, someone else will.

Powerful Takeaways

- Aristotle's rhetorical triangle includes logos (logic), pathos (emotion), and ethos (credibility).
- Aristotle offered two now often forgotten emotional appeals. Kairos is about relevance and taking advantage of the right moment to deliver a message. Telos is the end game, the purpose, the essential aim of a speech, a sales pitch, or a presentation. It's the point you hope to convey to your audience.
- The brain's reticular activating system is responsible for filtering through the clutter that bombards all of us. Therefore, as communicators and influencers we must learn to appeal to someone's RAS to gain their attention and to influence an outcome. Stories do that.
- The best leaders are teachers, mentors, and role models—and they accomplish the majority of their work through influence, not authority.

3

Sequence Is EVERYTHING

"The true measure of leadership is influence . . . nothing more, nothing less."

—John C. Maxwell, author of
The 21 Irrefutable Laws of Leadership[1]

SEQUENCE—THE ORDER OF things—plays a major role in how effectively we influence others. It's a driver of whether the audience gets the message, takes it to heart, and then acts on or rejects it.

Ideas are like seeds. If planted correctly in properly tilled soil and nurtured—the sequence—they will take root and grow. You wouldn't plant a seed in cement or drop it on top of the soil and never nurture it. Yet that's how most people share their ideas. We must accept the reality that there is a sequence to how people process information and more importantly, accept ideas. Spouting logic, data, and facts alone doesn't cut it, yet we still gravitate to that behavior.

To maximize the power of influence requires understanding the applications and underpinnings of how sequencing affects the way we process and embrace information.

A Matter of Patterns

Sure, there's a beginning, middle, and end to every story, but beyond that when a message follows the right sequence, it's easier to understand and repeat. At some time in our lives—perhaps in school or before a sales call—all of us have had to memorize a list of something and arrange the words, names, or numbers in an order that made them easier to remember. That's a kind of sequencing.

Educators use sequence to help their students understand and organize learning as well as solve problems. A sequence can be a list as mentioned above, steps to follow and in what order, a historical timeline, an unfolding plot, or a series of events.[2] Computer programmers write code in sequence, the logical order for a computer to understand.

For the purpose of this book, sequence is positioning your message and delivery of a message, story, or presentation in a way that aligns with the biological and neurological makeup of how our brains are wired to receive it. What's more, when we add the idea of getting our hearts to speak in that neurological sequence, we can achieve the ultimate goal of maximum connection and impact.

Successful communicators intuitively use this kind of sequence. But for many people, this is a new kind of sequence. At first it may feel counterintuitive and at times paradoxical. But once understood, the AMPLIFII sequence—the formula for delivering an influential message—will explain many previously confusing or mysterious aspects of life, seriously. My goal is for you to understand this sequence explicitly and be able to replicate it consistently.

The Three P's: Predict, Preempt, Prevent

One of my favorite things about human behavior is that when we understand and pay attention to it, a lot is predicable. Many of us already are relatively good at predicting people's responses to messages, but we usually don't take the time to go through the exercise.

Stop and Think

Too often leaders and communicators fail to think through how an audience might respond to a message before they ever deliver it. Instead, they are focused on what they want to say and how they want to say it.

This also is a central component in emotional intelligence (EQ) that we explored earlier—the ability to understand an audience's emotional responses to a message before it's delivered. This is another example of the role that our brain's prefrontal cortex—our future simulator—plays in our day-to-day lives.

Next time you craft a message, take a moment to ask yourself if there is anything about that message that might trigger resistance. If there is, think about what you can you do to preempt that response to prevent it.

Predicting Resistance

I've led many strategic planning sessions for leadership teams, and a key message I always deliver is that there will be some resistance to the decisions they make.

Leaders planning for change perceive their decisions as the next logical steps or strategic moves. But those who receive the information recognize it as something different and potentially scary—change. Many leaders forget that and are surprised when their people aren't as excited by the plans as they are.

A good approach to soften resistance to change is the three Ps mentioned earlier. First, *predict* what part of the plan will face the greatest resistance and by whom. That will allow preparation for and implementation of a *preemptive* strategy to *prevent* or reduce the resistance.

Often that preemptive strategy involves as little as a few conversations with key people before announcing a change. That gives others a chance to respond to the plan or provide additional input. Getting buy-in before an announcement is a good strategy versus waiting to see how those affected respond.

If more than a conversation is required, then the team may need to look at who is delivering the message. If it is a high-profile change, it may require the CEO to deliver the message to illustrate its importance. This strategy works best in conjunction with common sense and trusting your gut. Identify the resistance points. Put the best people in place to deliver the message.

Lastly, a preemptive strategy is usually best executed through a powerful story that helps the team understand the purpose for the needed changes. A story and delivery style that honors those people facing change and acknowledges their inevitable stress goes a long way toward gaining buy-in and trust from everyone involved.

The Big Mistake

The wrong sequence is one of the biggest mistakes people make when they communicate. When we're asked a question, the tendency is to answer in the here and now with no context or framing. When that happens, the brain is forced to create its own frame of reference based on past experience to fill in the gap of knowledge, and there is no telling whether that will help or hurt the intended meaning of the message. The brain is not able to deal with not having a frame as that is how it constructs reality. Professionals were taught to be direct, concise, matter-of-fact, and to the point. Unfortunately, that leaves a lot of room for assumption.

Control the Message

Instead, think about trying a different sequence by sharing a more complete story and leaving little to the listener's imagination. Instead of the time sequence of here and now, we can draw on the past and the future to answer a question; we can create context that connects with our audience. Think of the connection created by the right sequence as preparing the audience—opening their minds and piquing their interest—for the message to be delivered and then acted on.

Consider these two different answers to the same question:

"Who are you; what do you do, and what makes you unique?"

Answer A: My name is John. I'm a mortgage banker. I got into this business because I like to educate people. I learned that from my dad.

John answered the question exactly how it was asked. It's clear. We now know who John is, what he does, and he briefly touched on what he felt was unique. The problem is that most people in his industry also like to educate people, so his answer did little to set him apart or add any unique value.

As the audience, do we care to listen to what else John wants to say after a pitch like his? Probably not, because John made no impact on us. He answered matter-of-factly and in the here and now—out of sequence.

Now read the second answer. Think about how you feel as you read it. How do those feelings differ from any feelings you might have had with John's first answer?

Answer B: Growing up in my family, education was everything, especially to my dad. But I wasn't a very good student. In fact, at the time, my buddies and I had this bright idea to quit school, get jobs, and make some real money.

When I told my dad the plan and that it involved leaving school, he was furious. He picked up the phone, called the school principal, pulled me out of that school immediately, and enrolled me in another school a half-hour away. At that moment I hated my dad for taking me so far away from my friends.

It wasn't until a year later that I realized that my dad had actually saved my life. My friends who had dropped out, one was in a dead-end job, the second was into drugs, and the third one was in jail. I was on my way to college.

My dad had given me the best gift ever—education and the power of choice. I knew at that moment that no matter what work I did, I wanted to educate people. I wanted to give them the same gift that my father gave me.

When I was introduced to the mortgage and real estate business, I saw an industry that needed people to help educate clients. To sit with them and help them navigate a complex process, educating them so they could make better decisions for their lives. So here I am today. I'm proud to say that every single day of my career, I can give the gift of education to my clients as a mortgage banker. And I love it.

Yes, some might typically refer to this answer as long-winded. But now the audience knows who John is, the passion and value he brings to the table, and why he is so good at what he does—John's origin story (more on that later).

By answering in this sequence—drawing on the past to explain the present and into the future, instead of solely the here and now—John has connected emotionally with his audience. He's told a story with the AMPLIFII formula—frame, message, tie-down.

The feeling—the emotion—we get from John's long story about who he is, what his work is, and the story of his passion's origins creates a very different response in his audience. That same feeling is what we as communicators strive for in our audiences. Think of your message delivery in the same manner. Strive to connect with your audiences in the right sequence.

Questioning Questions

To be able to deliver a moving answer like John's that properly influences an audience, we first must unlearn some old habits related to questions.

- **Most people don't put much thought into the questions they ask.**

  Have you ever asked someone how they are doing and when they answered, realized it didn't really matter? You didn't really want to know. You were just making small talk and speaking out of habit. The one who asks isn't really interested in knowing, and the person who responds isn't telling the truth. Following that scenario, there is a missed chance and a meaningless discussion with no connection.

  The same thing happens with most questions in business settings. The questions and answers people really want to know are often hidden deeper in conversations and unintentionally masked by surface, shallow questions such as, "So what do you do?" What someone really is asking is, "Tell me something interesting about you because I don't know what else to ask."

- **We feel an overwhelming obligation to answer questions asked of us.**

  I received a phone call from an executive who asked me to help her company deal with a question that kept coming up. The company was in transition, the CEO had just left, and they were worried this executive was going to leave as well. She shared that many of her staff kept asking if she was going to leave and what her plans were. She felt that by not answering them she was lying.

I asked if she knew her plan, and she said she didn't. Then I asked if she thought that people are entitled to an answer to the questions they ask. She said she did. So I asked when was the last time she had sex. Obviously, she was shocked and immediately said she didn't need to answer that question, which illustrated my point. Just because I asked a question, doesn't mean I am entitled to an answer. She laughed and said, "When you put it like that, it makes sense."

I also pointed out that those questions had nothing to do with her well-being or future. Instead, they serve the needs of those asking the questions.

So we crafted an honest answer that refocused the conversation on what mattered most—the business. The new response:

"John (the name of whoever asks the question), the company is in a lot of transition, and I honestly don't know what I am going to do. But I do know this. The company needs both of us to focus on the business right now. What do you need from me to help you stay focused?"

This question redirected the conversation to creating value for the company and showed that its CEO was there to support the team and empower the individual to ask for help.

- **The person asking the questions is in control.**

Questions are powerful because they set the frame of the conversation. By setting the frame, you control the direction of the conversation, which can be advantageous. By throwing out a topic and leading the listener to reply to your views, you get complete control over the conversation.

Most professionals know this intellectually but still get caught up in answering questions that don't set them up in a strong strategic position.

To sum up, the result is that we humans feel compelled to answer questions that people put little thought into and that give them control of the narrative. The moment someone asks the price, the rate, or the commission before you've had a chance to communicate value, it's over.

If you're presenting a budget or a plan that has complexities, and people ask you to "get to the bottom line," you run the risk of not fully communicating the value proposition in the right context.

From that perspective, it's easy to see the risk in blindly, succinctly answering questions. Instead, sometimes we need to question the questions being asked of us and look beyond to deliver an answer that adds value.

In Tune

Before delivering any message, we must be in tune with the emotions of our audience. If a message has the potential to trigger a negative or stressful emotional state and threatens the audience's ability to hear the message, then use a preemptive strategy to calm those emotions.

And do it before ever sharing the message. That's how I addressed and connected with the audience whose company had just been sold as mentioned in Chapter 2.

It's about preparing the listener—opening their minds to— the message. Speaking from the heart—values, beliefs, and memories through story—can be our biggest source of influence. When our hearts begin to speak, we and our audience begin to open up because we create safety and lay the groundwork for trust.

Brain scans show that our brains and those of our audience actually begin to mirror one another as we create connection and rapport. We'll dive deeper into that neural coupling and story-telling later.

Influence is not about sounding good or being a polished speaker. It's about getting people to trust you and act on your ideas. The fastest way to get that to happen is through connection to your story. But for the audience to connect with the story, you first must connect with the story. An audience can immediately tell if the story means anything to you or if you are just reciting bullet points of an event. If you connect from the heart, your audience will connect, too. That's why it's so important to make it personal, and if possible, vulnerable.

Preempt any negatives, too, before they come up in thought or discussions. Again, that's how in my keynote I addressed and connected with the audience whose company had just been sold.

All the best speakers—from leaders to actors to influencers—follow certain sequence in their speeches. Civil rights leader Martin Luther King Jr. was a master at evoking passion to set his audience up for his message. His vision for a better world still captures our attention and inspires us to take action.

Adversity and Memory

Not all of us are as gifted as Dr. King. But that doesn't mean we shouldn't set our sights on goals more attainable and immediately acted on. The good news is that each of us has the ability to connect and inspire people with our own stories. The problem, though, is most people don't think they have much of a story to share. That's because our story is all we know. Our struggles are simply part of our daily experiences.

The most resilient leaders have incredible coping skills to get through adversity. One of those skills is the ability to not dwell on the struggles of life. Although that skill works great when someone is pushing through difficult times, it's not so good when it comes time to share the stories of struggle. Often when these leaders share their past, they brush over the struggles as if nothing really happened and in the process miss the opportunity to connect with others who may have gone through something similar.

The Brain and Sequence

The brain is a complex machine, the nerve center for how we humans operate and who we are. The 1990s were coined the Decade of the Brain by then President George H.W. Bush in an effort to enhance public awareness of the benefits from brain research. More was discovered in those 10 years than in all of history.

These few pages certainly aren't enough to provide a full understanding of all the complexities of the brain, nor would all that information really be valuable from the perspective of influence. Instead, we will focus on the practical application of the research and how it can help improve our lives in the areas of leadership, communication, sales, change, influence, events, and our families.

Our brains process information in certain sequences. Once we recognize those sequences, we can better understand how we embrace some new ideas and innovations and why we resist others.

In other words, why we resist or accept change. The goal is to align our messages to work with our audience's brains rather than against them, allowing for faster acceptance. After all, everything we do in sales, leadership, communication, parenting, and more usually involves some sort of change.

The brain has two primary functions. First, it protects us from the threat of death so we can continue to live and procreate. Second, the brain makes sense of all the sensory inputs we receive. But even those functions have a sequence.

Nerve Signals Travel Faster Than Hormones

When it comes to self-preservation, the brain decides the fight-or-flight response. That response is controlled by the amygdala, a walnut-shaped part of the brain that monitors sensory inputs for signs of threat. In essence, the amygdala is our panic button. If it senses a shark, for example, someone pointing a gun in our direction, or, in my case, a bee (I have a bee phobia), it has seconds or even a split second to organize the body's organs to send blood to muscles for defense.

The amygdala does that with the help of a connection to the thalamus, which is the brain's relay station. Think of the thalamus as New York City's Grand Central Terminal.

Together the amygdala and the thalamus must organize all the gathered sensory information to orchestrate a response to defend (fight) or flee (flight), or in some instances take no action (freeze). This happens efficiently because of the connection to the hypothalamus, which is in the middle of the brain and in charge of regulating our autonomic functions, including breathing, digestion, and heartbeat.

The hypothalamus is connected directly to the autonomic nervous system, which controls the parasympathetic (calm response) and sympathetic (excited response) nervous systems. Those two opposing nervous systems are antagonistic, which means they can't function at the same time. These are nerve signals, not hormonal signals triggered by emotions. All this happens before we are even consciously aware that anything happened or might happen.

That is a lot to digest, but it's essential to understanding influence. Our messages must be structured in a sequence that aligns with this biological and neurological reality; otherwise, we have no chance of our messages being heard.

Why Does It Matter?

Keep in mind that these behind-the-scenes brain connections happen before our neocortex even processes the idea of a potential threat. In other words, your brain already is prepared to fight before you are consciously aware of a threat.

That's important because your brain interprets the threat of change, new ideas, the sale of a company, a verbal attack, and so much more in the same way it interprets a physical threat. Put another way, your message or attempt to influence has the ability to trigger the fight/flight/freeze response in your audience. That's a concept most people don't realize. And if you ignore the concept, your message has no chance of connecting with your audience.

Four Steps to Influence

Our brain shuts down to new ideas under stress. There is a sequence that helps calm the primitive defensive mechanisms that get in the way of change, innovation, relationships, conflict resolution, presentations, and selling.

Over the last 30 years, we have trained more than 100,000 people in some hostile work environments, including union/labor issues, mergers and acquisitions, hostile takeovers, and entitled sales teams. Every workshop or training session we design follows these four steps to prevent the defensive parts of the brain from sabotaging the work while fostering engagement.

Step 1: Am I Safe?

As mentioned earlier, the first job of the brain is to keep us alive, which is why the amygdala constantly searches for threats. Those threats are measured by stress levels that can be caused by physical as well as psychological threats. The latter include fear of judgment, ridicule, embarrassment, criticism, job loss, change, public speaking, and the list goes on and on.

The hypothalamus is the area of the brain that oversees our autonomic functions such as breathing, digestion, and fear—flight/fight/freeze aspect of humans. There's no logic, reason, or understanding involved. Only one question concerns the hypothalamus: "Am I safe?" If that question can't be answered or is, "No," then the brain will not be open to new ideas, change, or influence.

When someone is caught in the "am I safe" mode, it is not the time to sell an idea or try to convince them of anything. This is the time for listening, structure, and predictability, which all begin the process of creating psychological safety.

That safety is the ability to show and employ oneself without fear of negative consequences on self-image, status, or career, according to William A. Kahn, professor of management and organizations, Questrom School of Business at Boston University.[3]

This psychological safety can be defined as a shared belief that the team is safe. Remember, the brain responds in the same manner to psychological threats as it does to physical ones; it shuts down.

When it comes to our audiences, we can encourage the feeling of psychological safety by making people feel comfortable voicing their opinions without fear of being judged. For example, in a business situation, helping teams develop a safe environment for discussion could include creating ground rules for interaction. No interrupting others when they are talking is a good starting point.

The well-known approach to brainstorming—there are no bad ideas—is an example of creating safety. That's because a critical environment causes stress and shuts down the creative parts of the brain.

For a leader, psychological safety also could mean ensuring that a team is part of the decision-making process by listening to the team's needs and tailoring the message with those needs in mind.

The best way to create safety is to establish structure, order, and predictability. Agendas in meetings, rituals, standard practices, handshakes, and consistency are all examples of things that create a feeling of safety. Without that feeling, the brain isn't open to listening or to accepting new ideas.

To encourage psychological safety and connect with my audience, I make every attempt to take the time to meet and shake hands with them before I begin my speech or presentation. It's time-consuming but well worth it to put my audience at ease. (Incidentally, this helps put me at ease, too, no matter the size of the audience.) At a recent conference I shook hands with nearly 500 people before going on stage to give my keynote address. It was all worth it when I took to the stage and saw all those smiling faces. I had already made the connection before ever beginning my presentation.

Step 2: Do You Care About Me?

After someone feels safe, the next step is to ensure they feel valued. The absence of feeling valued creates more stress, which leads to the cortical inhibition we want to avoid. The limbic system controls our emotions and our memory as well as our values. All of us have met a person and immediately forgotten their name. That likely is because your limbic system wasn't fully engaged and was still at some level assessing the safety of the situation.

The limbic system is a very small part of the brain, but when engaged in making decisions, it has 35,000 times more neurons firing than the part of our brain that handles logic.

Have you ever tried to talk someone out of being in love with the wrong person? Or what about trying to change their political minds? It's a seemingly impossible task with biology working against you.

That's why branding firms focus so heavily on eliciting emotions and values. And that's why political campaigns trigger anger and hate because all those neurons can move people to lose sight of logic and vote a certain way.

The limbic system is an open-loop system—it is affected by outside influences. A smile from someone has an impact on us, and so does the sight of a puppy or the right words at the right time. This is the part of the brain that allows us to connect to our audiences and is essential to influence.

This also is the part of the brain that asks, "Do you care about or value me?" It's the part of the brain that is primed for relationship and rapport building. It actually buys your product. The challenge is that since this part of the brain makes decisions based on emotion, when the emotion wears off, it needs logic to reinforce the decision. If there is no logic, then we find ourselves in buyer's remorse.

Go back to the fundamental things we learned in school and from our parents. Listening, eye contact, smiles, and validation are simple ways to value people. Starting the meeting with a "check-in" to give everyone a chance to speak is also a way of saying, "We value you enough to stop the meeting to hear you." Ending with a "checkout" not only values people but also reinforces the key messages and takeaways from the meeting.

Step 3: Is This Engaging?

Now that we have our audience's attention, we need to keep it by not being boring. We do that by fluctuating between stimuli and novelty. And that means more brain science. The cerebral cortex is the brain's center for learning, logic, and language. It is the target area for problem solving and creativity. This part of the brain loves data, the search for truth, language, problem solving, value propositions, new ideas, and innovation.

The first time you see the "check engine" light appear, it captures your attention. Then after about a week, you don't even notice it anymore because the stimulus hasn't changed and our attention moves on to other, more stimulating things.

Novelty triggers dopamine, and tension triggers norepinephrine, the two neurotransmitters needed to capture attention. This is where many people lost their audiences during the pandemic and virtual meetings. The presenters were boring talking heads that never moved. TV shows and movies use novelty and tension to keep our attention and also get us to return the next week.

As a speaker/potential influencer, the Neocortex part of the brain is the target for your messages. But if the audience doesn't feel safe or they don't feel you care about them—the connection—then this part of the brain has a tough time engaging. That's because blood flow has been redirected to the parts of the body needed for protection. Blood flowing freely to the brain allows neurons to fire and engage with new ideas while painting pictures of possibility. That can't happen under stress.

In a business setting, the use of visuals, colors, video, powerful music, dynamic voice inflection, and body movement all contribute to making things more engaging. The goal is to keep the audience's attention.

Step 4: Is This Inspiring?

The final step is to engage the brain's prefrontal lobe to align future actions with personal values.

The prefrontal cortex is the CEO or the executive center of the brain, and so it determines future actions. Another way to think about it is as a future simulator. It is the last part of the brain to develop—usually not fully until age 25. This part of the brain constantly creates scenarios and looks to the future.

Imagine that a friend invited you to their house for homemade ice cream. Specifically, the friend wanted you to try a new flavor—liver and onions. Would you try it? Most likely your answer is a hard no! That's because your future simulator—the prefrontal lobe—drew from past experiences, assimilated them, and enabled you to imagine the potential taste of liver and onion ice cream. The simulator might have even provided a visceral response to the thought of liver and onion ice cream.

Especially fascinating about the prefrontal lobe is how it connects to the limbic system when trying to decide your next move. That connection determines if the move is aligned with your values. If it's aligned, you act; if not, you don't. That's yet another important reason to connect with your audience and appeal to their personal values.

Money will go only so far, but when values are engaged, we will stop at nothing. As an extreme example, I could offer you any sum of money to jump into shark-infested waters, and, most likely, you wouldn't go in. But if your child or a dear loved one fell in, you would be in those waters to save them without a second thought.

It is the same cortical connection that drives a passionate company culture, exciting new start-up, and volunteer mission trip. My company was named after this phenomenon, Volentum. Volentum is actually a Latin word meaning "to be wishing and willing." I came across it by combining the words *voluntary* and *momentum*. Voluntary momentum is when our voluntary energy is pointed toward a goal. It is a very powerful force, and all the methodologies in this book are geared to attract that energy.

Not All Audiences Are the Same

Presentation sequence matters, too. Sometimes different cultures and demographics also have different sequences. Some cultures consider discussing business immediately on arrival as rude and as indicating a lack of trustworthiness. As a presenter, ignoring that cultural bias means no chance of getting the deal. That's why we need to understand the sequence of our intended audience and align our message accordingly.

In most cases starting with the message and value proposition doesn't work, either. Remember, structure, order, and predictability create safety and security.

On the other hand, if the pitch is to raise money from venture capitalists, the sequence follows an expected protocol—the numbers first and story second. Think of the popular television show *Shark Tank*. In that scenario, the sequence goes something like this: "Hi, we are (company name), and we are seeking so many dollars in exchange for this much stake in our company."

Then the speakers pitch a good story that defines the problem and the solution—the product for which they seek capital. Often, though, contestants will have a great story with ethos (credibility) and strong pathos (emotion) but lack logos (logic). When that happens, forget raising capital.

Personal Values

To master the art and science of influence, we must immerse ourselves in understanding not only our personal values and the values of our audience but also the role those values play in our lives. Some experts say our personal values are formed somewhere between the ages of 9 and 13 and are pretty much locked in by age 21. (This time period is important to remember, especially when it comes to uncovering your origin story. More on that later.) That means by the time most of us enter the workforce, our values are difficult, if not impossible, to change.

We see so many leaders try to *change* people's values. The thought is, "We have to get them to value X." That's tough to do unless some traumatic event occurs that works to change those values. Adding to the disconnect, there's a high probability that those people already value something similar or congruent to "X." Values don't really change, but they do reprioritize as we age. There are stages in life when family is a higher priority, and there are events that cause a shift in priorities. Tragedy, health scares, new romantic relationships, all have the ability to affect our priorities.

Unfortunately, accessing (neurologically) those values is difficult because the environment in which a leader is trying to influence is not *safe*. The audience doesn't feel psychologically *safe*, and as we discussed, without that security, influence doesn't happen. That matters when it comes to influence because if we can align our message with what the audience already values, then they will most likely fully engage with the speaker and their message.

This is another opportunity to become a student of your own experience. Think about the values that are essential to you, those things that matter in your life. Perhaps honesty, family, and financial freedom stand out. Why do they stand out? Who were your coaches and role models when you were ages 9 to 13, those formative years? Often, personal values come from those years and those role models. Most likely those role models either exhibited those values well or you needed those values and those role models failed you, so you chose them as your own.

When your message can connect with the areas of the brain that control emotion, values, and logic, people buy into that message because it aligns with what they believe in. The result is influence. I think of it in terms of the head and heart uniting in action.

Powerful Takeaways

- Before delivering any message, we must be in tune with the emotions of our audience.
- Think ahead of time how an audience might respond to a message.

- Our brains process information in certain sequences. The goal is to align our messages to work with our audience's brains rather than against them, allowing for faster acceptance.
- The four elements an audience considers when it comes to influence include:
    - Am I safe?
    - Do you care?
    - Is this engaging?
    - Is this inspiring?
- Your message should consider the sequence and culture of an intended audience.
- The brain responds to psychological threats the same way as it does to physical ones; it shuts down.
- Your audience must feel psychologically *safe* because without that security, influence doesn't happen. Structure, order, and predictability create that safety and security.

4

Self-Awareness and Discovery

"The unexamined life is not worth living."

—Socrates

MOST CONVERSATIONS ABOUT influence revolve around Jedi mind tricks, persuasion, and delivering a keynote speech to a large crowd. Those conversations are interesting but not really related to the work of becoming a powerful influencer. That work begins inside each of us.

The No. 1 skill of a leader is self-awareness. Every reputable leadership course teaches it, and every top leader exhibits it. Self-awareness is the power that enables us to effect change in our own lives and the lives of those around us.

A Closer Look

Self-awareness is more than the ability to understand how our behavior and actions affect others. It is about identifying personal idiosyncrasies, those characteristics that we assume are the norm but which actually represent the exception.

The Disconnect

These idiosyncrasies are important because when there is a disconnect, a leader cannot connect with their teams or a speaker cannot connect with their audiences. For example, a speaker gives trite advice from a stage such as, "Just move on" or "Get over it," and the audience cheers.

Often, the speaker doesn't take into account that not everyone has the same ability to overcome or simply move on from adversity. Even worse, some people in the audience might not have those options. When that happens, the speaker comes across as tone-deaf—oblivious to the real feelings of their audience.

The Bottom Line

Self-awareness isn't just a soft skill. It has a significant impact on a company's bottom line. Employees at poor-performing companies, as measured by stock performance, were 79 percent more likely to have low overall self-awareness than those at firms with solid rates of return. That's according to research from Korn Ferry, a global organizational consulting firm.[1]

Even with scientific data supporting the importance of self-awareness, it remains an elusive skill for many in the workplace. Women in executive-level management positions are more self-aware than men in those same positions, according to the Hay Group—19 percent for women versus only 4 percent for their male counterparts.[2]

The Two Types

Over the years, many experts and not so experts have defined and studied self-awareness. One expert who has done exhaustive research on the topic is organizational psychologist and researcher

Tasha Eurich, PhD. She's the author of *Insight: The Surprising Truth About How Others See Us, How We See Ourselves, and Why the Answers Matter More Than We Think.*

In her popular 2017 Ted Talk, Eurich shares that people who are self-aware are better communicators, do better at work, and are more effective leaders at more profitable companies.[3] Incidentally, Eurich has a free self-awareness quiz online. It's not the be-all and end-all, but it does give insight into who we are (http://www.insight-quiz.com/selfquiz.aspx?z=0).

Eurich identified two categories of self-awareness—internal and external.[4]

Internal Self-Awareness

Internal self-awareness is how we see ourselves in relation to our values, emotions, strengths, weaknesses, and environment. Eurich found that internal self-awareness has a positive association with work and relationship satisfaction, perceived levels of self-control, creativity, and general happiness.[5] These skills all are essential for influence and success in life both personally and professionally.

External Self-Awareness

External self-awareness expresses how others see us in relation to our values, emotions, strengths, weaknesses, and environment. This is key to the skill of influence because it enables you to see yourself as others do.

Externally self-aware leaders are more empathetic and can better relate to others. Eurich's research also showed the organizational value of self-awareness in terms of greater job satisfaction, higher-performing employees, and greater productivity.[6]

> *"Follow those who seek the truth, run from those who claim they've found it."*
>
> — *Voltaire*

Warning: Self-Awareness Is Rare

Most people think they are relatively self-aware. But just because someone says or thinks it doesn't mean they are.

Only 10 to 15 percent of people who say they are self-aware really are, according to Eurich.[7] Putting that into perspective, the numbers mean that one of every ten leaders and managers fits the criteria of being self-aware. Let that sink in.

After studying the brain for as long as I have, one thing is clear: There is no way I know everything or have seen all the angles. I need multiple perspectives to even begin to understand a problem clearly. Sure, we can be confident in how we see things. But we also need to keep an open mind to the possibility of new information that could be useful or even that our view is just plain wrong. Truth is what matters most and is the measure of success.

What makes achieving true self-awareness even more difficult is that Eurich's research also found that experience and power hinder our self-awareness. So the smarter you are and the more successful you become, the more difficult self-awareness can be.

That's why it's important to focus on self-awareness. Anyone can learn the skill of influence, but if we lose sight of how our behaviors affect those around us, those skills are for nothing. No skill or technique will make up for a lack of judgment or being tone-deaf.

On the other hand, a self-aware leader has the power to inspire us to effect change in our own lives and the lives of those around us. People who are self-aware understand their why as well as the what when it comes to action and belief in themselves and others.

Your Experiences

When we understand the why behind the action, it's much easier to understand and trigger the same feelings and actions in others. Again, it begins with becoming a student of your own experiences.

That means being mindful of interactions with people, how they behave, and how you feel about it and being mindful about how you behave, what you say, and how others might respond. Pay attention to repeated feedback from others; it's a sign to heed. Pay particular attention to the feedback if it makes you feel defensive. That feedback could be closer to a truth you're unwilling to face.

Also, pay attention to yourself and how you feel and to others and how they feel. Learning from our experiences isn't always a given. It requires a conscious and ongoing effort. We all have our lapses in learning. That's just human nature. But we must always keep trying.

Successful leaders are consciously in touch with who they are, their emotions, and what's happening around them. Without that awareness, a person is disconnected and has minimal influence. He or she can speak, but no one listens; no one is inspired, and that person commands little respect.

For example, consider Johnny. He means well, but he just doesn't get it and seems to lack any connection with the general sentiment around him or how people feel. He makes jokes at the wrong times and tries to inspire when he should just listen.

Johnny posts on social media about the need to quarantine while he's sitting in his hot tub with his perfect family. It never occurs to him that many people don't have hot tubs or can't be home with their families. He definitely doesn't realize that some people can't afford to stop working and go home, as he can.

Johnny means well, but he ends up hurting and frustrating others. Sadly, no one will tell him, though, because they know how he'll respond. The opposite of Tone-Deaf Johnny is someone who is empathetic.

Presence

Self-awareness also is about how you present yourself to others. Olivia is articulate, wise, and has a beautiful smile that can light up a room. But few people know that. It's not because Olivia doesn't have a great message to tell; she does. She's self-aware on many levels, but Olivia seldom speaks up.

Sound familiar? So many people have powerful messages to share but for one reason or another aren't willing to step up and step out into the limelight. Perhaps it's shyness—the freeze response—or the fight-or-flight response linked to criticism or fear of making a mistake, or even insecurities leftover from childhood.

Whatever the reason, if we choose the path of becoming more influential, we need to begin the process of addressing everything that might be stopping us from getting in the game.

As leaders, people are watching us whether we like it or not. We have to AMPLIFII our level of self-awareness to include body language, facial expressions, and the behavior of actually speaking up. A diamond in the rough like Olivia can't influence anyone by staying in the corner. She has to come out and get in the game.

Conversely, I'm six feet, three inches tall, bald, have a goatee, and weigh around 260 pounds. I have the advantage of being physically larger than many people, which makes it harder to miss me when I enter a room. That said, I have been to events where I felt completely invisible. When I first started as a speaker, I would walk into a room and not a single person would acknowledge or speak to me.

Then I would take the stage, and for the rest of the convention, people would talk to me nonstop. That power of being on stage and the immediate influence it created fascinated me.

You're On

I speak regularly to thousands of people. However, the way I walk into a room still matters. Each of us must learn to be self-aware of how we move in order to control our body language so we can deliver the right message.

We need to learn how to be gracious and grateful (yes, men can be graceful, too), confident and poised, willing to step up and out to deliver our messages and be approachable afterward. It's all part of true self-awareness and understanding all the gifts each of us has to share.

Remember, we communicate with our bodies before we do with our mouths, so make sure your body screams the right message.

Value in Practice

Like influence, self-awareness is a skill that can be learned. And also like influence, it takes time and conscious effort as well as practice. Just like any skill worth developing or any craft worth mastering, you'll need to devote years of discipline and practice to honing your abilities.

That may sound daunting, but those years will pass even if you don't practice these skills. So why not find yourself in five to ten years with five to ten years of practice and discipline under your belt? You won't regret it; I promise.

Train like the Elite Professionals

I have had the fortunate opportunity to work with elite athletes, Navy SEALs, and CEOs. The one thing that unequivocally separates these top performers from amateurs is the intensity of how they train.

Think about a professional athlete. The intensity of their training is tough for some of us to fathom. Everything is at game speed and drenched in sweat. It's nonstop, and they're always working to become better at what they do.

Whether it's a basketball great, tennis or golf professional, Olympian, or a high school athlete, all work hard to improve their skills. So do musicians, chess champions, teachers, and poker players. They all practice to improve.

A speaker and influencer is no different—except maybe the part about drenched in sweat. We must put in years of research and countless hours of practice in front of the mirror, the camera, and on small stages to become better at not only speaking, giving presentations, and storytelling, but also at self-awareness so that one day we can finally nail it on that big stage.

Far from Perfect

But beware, practice does *not* make perfect. That's right. Practice makes consistent. If I have a bad golf swing and I continue to practice that bad swing over and over, I will have a consistently bad golf swing. Perfect practice makes perfect. That's why athletes—business leaders, too—have coaches to ensure that they practice perfectly.

Feedback with an outside perspective is invaluable in the process of building self-awareness because people in general vastly overinflate their personal competence. In other words, we tend to think we're a lot smarter and better equipped to handle life and its curveballs than we really are. We tend to judge others by their worst actions and ourselves by our best intentions.

Discovery

The better we understand ourselves and how and why we react to certain things, the better we can channel and connect with influence.

Are You Self-Aware?

Individuals who are self-aware:

- *Know their strengths and weaknesses.*
- *Understand their personal values and are comfortable with them without outside influence.*
- *Are in touch with their emotions and feelings and the emotions and feelings of others.*
- *Are receptive to and appreciate feedback.*
- *Understand how others perceive them.*
- *Have a keen understanding of how their body language affects those around them and their message.*

Increase Your Self-Awareness

Now that we understand what self-awareness is and isn't and its role in influence, let's look at some tips on how to grow our own self-awareness. Of course, being a student of our own experiences is crucial.

Journaling

If you already journal, then kudos. You understand the incredible value of going back through what you have written and the process of self-reflection and what it can teach us about ourselves. This takes time and discipline, but the payoff is well worth it.

I am a big fan of *The Five-Minute Journal* (https://www .intelligentchange.com). It offers a simple morning routine that poses three simple questions. When we answer those questions, it starts the day right. There's also a night routine to reflect on the day's positive experiences and focus on how to craft a more fulfilling tomorrow. All this literally takes less than five minutes a day with the opportunity to spend more time with longer questions.

The process of beginning every day with intention is about choosing self-awareness. By ending the day with reflection, you learn and become a student of your day to improve for tomorrow. It doesn't get much easier than that.

Grow Your Emotional Intelligence (EQ)

Self-awareness, as mentioned earlier, is a core component of emotional intelligence (EQ). EQ is your ability to recognize and understand emotions in yourself and others and your ability to use this awareness to manage your behavior and relationships.

There are a number of EQ tests online as well as invaluable books and endless YouTube videos on the subject. Type "EQ" into a search engine and start exploring and learning.

I want to spark your curiosity in this area because it will help you in every aspect of life.

Keep in mind that, as with anything else available free online, free quiz results aren't always accurate but are a good starting point on your journey. Some of the EQ tests available online include:

* Greater Good Science Center, University of California-Berkeley (https://greatergood.berkeley.edu/quizzes/ei_quiz/ take_quiz)

* Global Leadership Foundation (http://globalleadership foundation.com/geit/eitest.html)

* Psychology Today (https://www.psychologytoday.com/us/tests/personality/emotional-intelligence-test)

Pay Attention to External Triggers

Keep a list of external factors that make you feel happy, sad, defensive, attracted, intrigued, fearful, and anything else positive or negative. Identify the triggers or indicators—negative and positive—of each.

Then pay attention to those same behaviors and how they cause others to behave toward you. How do you respond to these triggers? How do they respond back to you? Note all of this in your journal.

Elicit Feedback from Trusted Sources

When you allow feedback in, your empathy grows and you understand your impact on others. Feedback helps you identify personal blind spots, which if not addressed, can hinder your ability to influence.

The best speakers, presenters, and sales agents, no matter how experienced they are, always debrief their presentations—even if it's just making a few mental notes. They usually have someone in the audience taking notes on areas for improvement. The process of continual, incremental improvement is the key to success. Plus, the small changes are easier to digest.

Record Everything!

At least one day a week, every professional sports team reviews film not only of themselves but of their competition. In today's world such review is easy.

You can look at your work even if only on a phone recording. Analyze what you talked about, how you said it, the sequence you said it in, what landed well, what missed the mark, the nuances that worked, and what fell short. You'll be surprised at what you learn and how you can improve through this benefit of hindsight.

If you are on a virtual meeting, no problem. Record those as well. Some virtual meeting apps include the record option. Just make sure you inform meeting participants ahead of time as a courtesy.

Identify Your Core Values and Align Them With Your Behaviors

We all have core values that guide what we do. Some people are more aware of those values than others.

However, the more conscious awareness you can create around what you value, the easier it becomes to align your decisions and behaviors. You also will find that greater awareness makes it easier to identify when you are out of alignment and even out of alignment with your audience.

Practice Mindfulness

So many underperforming leaders use the ideas of meditation and mindfulness as punchlines. That's the first sign they have never faced a screaming crowd or a game-winning shot. Countless Olympic athletes and world champions practice some form of meditation or mindfulness.

Admittedly the way some people practice these tools can be a bit uncomfortable and tough for a business to handle. But don't allow a few unusual practices to spoil the true value of mindfulness and meditation.

Mindfulness or meditation, practiced for even 10 minutes a day, has been shown to increase focus and enable people to pay better attention to what is happening in the moment. This brain training also helps leaders become better listeners by allowing them to eliminate distractions. That includes worrying about prepping for the next meeting.

Powerful Takeaways

- Internal self-awareness is how we see ourselves in relation to our values, emotions, strengths, weaknesses, and environment.
- External self-awareness expresses how others see us in relation to our values, emotions, strengths, weaknesses, and environment. This is key to the skill of influence because it enables you to see yourself as others do.
- We need to learn how to be gracious and grateful (yes, men can be graceful, too), confident and poised, willing to step up and out to deliver our messages, and be approachable afterward.
- Practice doesn't make perfect. Perfect practice does. That's why athletes—business leaders, too—have coaches to ensure that they practice perfectly.
- Journaling is an excellent form of self-reflection that can teach us about ourselves and help us become better at what we do.
- Self-awareness is an important part of emotional intelligence.
- Conscious awareness helps us align our messages, decisions, and behaviors around our values.

PART

II

The Formula

5

Frames: Window into Your World

"You are either adding to or subtracting from your influence. There is no middle ground."

—René Rodriguez

FRAMES ARE CONSTRUCTS of reality that provide psychological context to help us understand our world. The more familiar terminology is *frame of reference*—the concept of drawing on past experience or knowledge to help understand something in our current reality.

For example, someone could have snow skied as a child and wiped out doing so. From then on, that wipeout is how they frame the experience of skiing and their behavioral responses to it. Their frame of that experience could include:

- trauma;
- fun;
- humiliation;
- what always happens to me;
- a natural part of life;
- feedback on how to improve.

The list of possible frames is endless. Someone who frames the experience as fun will respond much differently from someone who frames it as humiliating.

In communication, either the speaker provides the frame or the listener will provide one subconsciously. The listener has to since it's the only way we know how to perceive the world.

A Different Approach

To truly master the art and science of influence requires us to unlearn old habits. That includes ceasing to answer questions and deliver messages without first proper framing.

To better understand these changes, let's again think about sequence and how the brain processes information. Picture communication in the form of a timeline with past, present, and future. Most miscommunication happens because we answer in the here and now and without any context. When we assume that our listener operates from our same frames of reference, we risk being completely misunderstood.

To understand how frames construct reality, consider this example. If someone holds up a marking pen—one of those felt-tip markers available in a variety of colors—we know what it is because we've likely used one before. We all have the same frame of reference. Our past experiences help us understand what is in front of us. They are our construct of reality.

Sounds pretty simple. But let's take a deeper look.

What comes to mind when someone mentions the profession "used car salesman"? We likely think of words such as *sleazy* and *pushy* and think of someone out to rip us off. If the mention of a profession prompts ugly words like these, imagine the impact those negative frames can have on others.

"Don't worry. I'm a used car salesman. You can trust me." When I say that to an audience, most people laugh. The laughter is predictable because the words are incongruent to the triggered frame. (More on incongruencies later.)

Claiming the Frame

My grandfather lived in Cuba and was determined to get himself and his family to the United States and hopefully a better life. So he wrote a letter to then-US President Harry S. Truman. It said that if the president would bring him and his family to the United States, he would join the US military and fight for the United States. Somehow the letter reached the right person. They were moved—influenced—by it, and my grandfather, grandmother, aunt, and mother were brought to America. True to his word, my grandfather then joined the military.

Fast-forward eight years, and my grandfather and his family ended up in Homestead, Florida, poised to achieve the American dream. Today Homestead is a busy suburb 30 miles north of Miami. But back then there wasn't much there but Patrick Air Force Base.

At the time, my grandfather's American dream was about as far as he could walk. But one person especially believed in my grandfather and recognized what he had done for our country. He helped my grandfather get an older vehicle so he could expand his job search. That changed the trajectory of my grandfather's life, my mother's life, and ultimately my life. That person who believed in my grandfather was a used car salesman.

Did you notice how when reading the above, no negative frame popped into your mind? With that story, I'm claiming the frame. I'm painting the picture and filling in the blanks so the listener doesn't have to develop their own frame, which would have likely been negative. Either you provide the frame or your audience will provide one for you. Don't risk it; claim it.

Are you beginning to understand the importance of sequence and frame? Let's dissect the above frame. The revelation that the man who helped my grandfather was a used car salesman likely didn't elicit a negative response because it was in the context of the positive frame presented. In essence, I claimed the frame before your brain did. The back story about my grandfather created a frame that painted a picture of the person that far outweighed any negative past experiences with used car salesmen. Why? The answer is sequence. And I claimed the frame first.

The AMPLIFII Formula

The best and easiest way to understand how the three parts to the AMPLIFII formula—frame, message, tie-down—fit together is to see a real-life example. Then you will have a foundation to delve into the various elements.

The Janice Story

Janice was asked to interview for the role of president of a multibillion-dollar global conglomerate and brought my company in to help prepare her for an exhaustive job interview. Janice had a master's degree and a doctorate, and she carried herself with confidence and presence. When she spoke, everyone knew someone special was in the room. Actually, it was *her* room. In other words, she exuded massive ethos.

To help Janice prepare for the job interview, we staged a mock interview to assess as many aspects of her performance as possible. I sat off to the side to watch her facial expressions, micro-expressions, movements, sequencing, timing, and more.

One of the first questions the moderator asked was, "Tell us something you're most proud of in your life."

Janice thought a minute, and then responded confidently. "I earned straight A's my senior year in high school."

No Frame, Big Risk

The answer was short, concise, and to the point, just as every executive—most of us, too—has been taught. No fluff. That's great, right? Wrong!

Janice gave no frame, leaving the listeners to subconsciously try to understand what she meant. To do that, they draw on their own frames. The challenge is that Janice has no way of knowing what frames the listeners will choose and whether they will weigh in her favor or against it. That's not a good situation, whether it's in an interview, sales call, or presentation, because your ethos is at risk.

Perhaps various listeners framed Janice as lazy or a procrastinator who never bothered to study in high school until her senior year. Or maybe she was a spoiled kid who had everything handed to her so she didn't need to study.

Hearing those frames brought Janice to tears, an illustration of just how far off those frames were from her reality. Making Janice cry wasn't the intention. But it was a strong lesson for her to understand how easily a message can be lost when there's no frame provided. It also indicated the personal importance of her story.

When communicators don't set the stage or lay out a frame of reference for their audiences, that audience will fill in the narrative with their own ideas based on their experiences.

The Power of Framing

Leadership and influence aren't only about us speaking. More often they are about creating a platform for others to shine. This ability to listen for other people's values is critical in leadership.

Too often people listen from their own world and not that of their audience. Instead, when we listen to what is important to others and what they value, we can help them draw out important frames critical to better understand their message.

With the importance of frame in mind, Janice began to share more about why she was so proud of her grades her senior year:

> All my life everyone told me I was stupid and would never amount to anything. When you grow up hearing that all the time, you begin to believe it. I struggled in school. But something happened in my senior year of high school. I looked into the mirror and said, 'I'm either going to believe them forever or I'm going to do something about it and prove everyone wrong.' And I did do something. I got straight A's my senior year.

After Janice said that you could cut the emotion (pathos) in the room with a knife. One of the mock interviewers even wiped a tear because she felt so bad for misjudging Janice's initial answer. But that is simply how communication works. If we don't frame, our message is lost.

Stories Trigger Oxytocin

We now know that Janice is a fighter. She works hard to overcome the odds, and she is resilient. The frame captures our attention and aligns with our values. At the same time, it triggers a powerful domino effect of neurons in Janice's brain that couple with her audience's brain.

When that happens, our bodies secrete oxytocin, the hormone that triggers us to feel empathy. Empathy prepares us to take action. That's exactly what you want to happen in an interview. But what action? Enter the tie-down.

The story sets the frame and allows for Janice's message—that she's a resilient fighter—to be heard. It differentiates Janice from everyone else, and we're moved emotionally.

But we're not influenced just yet. We need the third and final piece of the AMPLIFII formula, the tie-down—where the value is created with a clear influence objective in mind.

The tie-down finishes the statement, *"What this means to you is . . . ."* It connects the dots of why this story is of value to the listener. It ensures that the listener doesn't assume incorrectly the moral or lesson of the story. It protects you from being misunderstood and makes the value you are delivering explicit and obvious. Never assume they see the value, tie it down.

Even though a tie-down sometimes is action-based, it's not necessarily a call to action. The tie-down is about clearly ensuring the value to the listener. Because the value is clearly connected to what matters to the listener, influence happens, action is taken, people get hired, products get purchased, and visions get followed.

With Janice, her influence objective was to get hired. That's clear, so her tie-down needs to make her story of overcoming struggles in school a reason she is the clear choice for this job.

Janice's full answer to the initial question using the AMPLIFII formula—frame, message, tie-down—looks like this:

1. **FRAME**: "Unfortunately, growing up I was surrounded by adults who told me I wasn't very smart. When adults tell you that as a child, you begin to believe it, and I had a hard time in school. But something happened in my senior year in high school. I looked at myself in the mirror and said, 'I'm either going to believe them forever or I'm going to do something about it and prove them wrong.' I decided I was going to do something about it. And I did."

2. **MESSAGE**: "I got straight A's my senior year."
3. **TIE-DOWN**: "I share that story with you because, if I do get the opportunity to work with you and your team, there will be times when we will be under pressure with our backs against the wall or facing seemingly insurmountable challenges. I promise you this: I'll be right out there working next to you as hard as I can to overcome the challenges in the same way I overcame challenges in my own personal life, but this time for you and your team."

Janice's message is clear. Her value is tangible. And her frame delivered with pathos makes it believable and causes us to want to act. That is influence.

Psychological Frame of Reference

Even more specifically, we need to think of frames as psychological frames of reference. A psychological frame is someone's frame of mind when they enter a situation, whether a sales presentation, classroom, training session, or first encounter.

Three factors figure into determining someone's perception:

- Physiological state;
- Past experience;
- Physical and emotional needs.

Those three factors also figure into the conversation about sequence. For example, someone may have an amazing idea to share, but if they haven't addressed someone's physiological reality, possible past negative experience, or their physical and emotional needs, the idea has no chance.

Perceptions

Our physiology affects how we perceive information. If we are blind, other senses are enhanced. If we are stressed, we are more defensive and skeptical to protect ourselves.

Our past experience is a powerful influence on our perception. At age 14 I was stung by 27 bees. Now, whenever I see a bee fly by out of the corner of my eye, my brain perceives it as a bee attack, and I react. Bad experiences prime us to anticipate and interpret a similar experience in a negative light.

These perceptions follow people into boardrooms and business as well. If someone grew up with their parents complaining about "management" and how badly they treated them or how they never listened, chances are that person's initial experiences with management will be negative or distrustful, too.

Positive Vibes

Conversely, a good experience tends to lead to a more positive perception and attitude in people. It also may keep people more relaxed, less defensive, or even more optimistic (to a fault) about a situation. This can be good but can also hurt as a good previous experience does not guarantee its repetition.

When it comes to physical or emotional needs, keep it simple. If you don't address them before you share your idea, pitch your product, or make your request, it's not happening. Remember, sequence is everything.

Keep in mind, too, that in the absence of a frame of reference from personal experience with a topic, person, or idea, an individual is open to being influenced by whoever provides the most compelling frame. If you have never met anyone outside of your culture, then your parents, coaches, friends, and even the media may influence how you perceive someone for the first time.

The same is true for political affiliations, the Android versus Apple debate, and religious preference. The goal is to build awareness around this phenomenon so that we can approach situations more intentionally.

Disruption Creates New Frames

Before Uber and Lyft, most people had no frame of reference for the concept of rideshare. Before Netflix and other streaming services, the widespread idea of watching any movie we wanted whenever we wanted was beyond reach for most people. Before Airbnb few people would allow a stranger to inhabit their private residence.

Now we don't think twice about any of these things because we understand the concepts. We have frames of reference and, more important, we trust the processes.

Many clients come to us for guidance because they want to craft and communicate messages that often are disruptive and lack frames of reference. So they end up sounding like everyone else. It's not easy to chart a new path and can require substantial time and money to do so successfully.

But, if successful, that brand might end up defining that space. Think Kleenex (tissues) and Xerox (copies), or more recently Airbnb, Uber, Netflix, and even Google, which has become a noun and a verb.

The Framing Battle

Everyone has an agenda, whether implicit or explicit. Businesses have products to sell. Each of us has projects to complete, strategies to execute, and many of us children to raise. Often those agendas are not initially aligned. That misalignment surfaces when two people or businesses need to work together, a consumer must choose a brand, or a voter has to choose a candidate.

The battle for attention, influence, and even financial resources is really a matter of whose frame is perceived as the most credible, compelling, and valuable. Because framing is a collection of concepts, metaphors, and theoretical references that together help us understand reality, story becomes a powerful device to control the narrative. But there are many other framing devices, too, including props, quotes, jokes, statistics, and even music. (More on that later.)

The battle of frames can be about whether something is valuable, whether it's a good or bad idea, whether there's a solution or not, or almost anything else that involves opposing viewpoints.

Whose frame will win on a sales call? Will the client dictate the frame or will the presenter? Will the audience see the presenter's frame as trite and clichéd or will they accept the frame as valid and valuable? That's why it's incumbent on all of us to invest the time and effort to hone our framing skills with the goal of achieving our influence objective.

Conscious and Subconscious

It's impossible to be consciously aware of all the frames we rely on to understand the world around us. Many of these frames subconsciously fill in the blanks when we're left without explanations.

Our perceptions of political parties, different ethnicities, the opposite sex, new technology, or a change in strategic direction are all affected by the frames through which we view them. Remember the used car salesman from earlier? Most people's initial image was that of someone obnoxious and sleazy, until I filled in the frame.

What unconscious frames does your profession trigger? What about your ideas or appearance? Instead of getting caught up in preconceived notions of others, get fascinated by and curious about the psychology and reality. When we let go of emotional or egocentric responses associated with a specific question or topic, we can become strategic about how we approach our message and preempt possible roadblocks.

I say this repeatedly because it's so important. If we don't frame things for our audience, our audience must build their own construct for understanding what's being said. The frame you present draws the audience in—grabs their attention—and can help them understand better the meaning of what you, the communicator/influencer, are attempting to convey.

Try the exercise below.

Apply the Learning: Framing

Think about this simple question, "What's your favorite color?" Consider the two different responses:

- *Answer A: green.*
- *Answer B: I was born in Miami, Florida. I spent the first 7 years of my life living in Miami, where I have such awesome memories of the palm trees, the beaches, the food, the music, and the culture. After that, I split my time between Miami and Minnesota until I was 16. Neither ever felt like home. But if I was on a beach and saw palm trees, I knew I was close to my friends, my family, my food, and my music—all the things that made me the happiest. Palm trees are green, so my favorite color is green.*

Now think about the two very different answers to the same question.

- **Answer A** is short, concise, and to the point—how we've been taught to deliver an answer. The answer adds zero value and fosters no connection.
- **Answer B.** When you read it, how did it make you feel? The frame likely generated a connection. If you like palm trees, beaches, Latin music, Cuban food, Miami, Minnesota, or might even be from a split home, you have made a connection. All this from a very simple question, "What's your favorite color?"
- **Of note:** Sometimes I share this example and someone says, "Just answer the color! I don't have time to say all that." My response to that: The second answer only took a few seconds longer than the first. And the purpose of the exercise is to unlearn an old habit of answering without a frame. Besides, if we're listening to several people sharing their favorite color, the only answer that likely will be remembered is mine (green). Not a bad return on investment (ROI) for a few more seconds of time invested in sharing. Don't forget, being remembered matters when it comes to referrals, branding, and positive reviews.

Think about the process of going back in time and adding that frame of reference. If you don't provide the frame, the listener will. Whatever the topic, that's the power of framing. Some more thoughts to consider:

- After being asked the question, think of the answer in your head (in this case, say the color to yourself) but NOT aloud.
- Ask yourself, again silently, "Why did I choose that answer (color)?"

- *Whatever story comes to mind, share it in detail.*
- *End the story with, ". . . and that's why (answer the question; in this case, 'My favorite color is . . .')"*
- *Don't give away the direct answer (the color) in the story. Keep the soft suspense until you reveal the answer at the end of your story.*
- *Use pathos (emotion) in the story by talking about your feelings related to the question/answer. For example, "I remember feeling a sense of . . ." or "I was so mesmerized by how they made me feel . . ."*
- *Use details. They draw in an audience and help them paint a picture. For example, "You could smell the lavender the moment you walked up to Gramma's house." Or "I remember picking up my son for the first time and being surprised by how heavy a newborn was; I almost dropped him!"*

Frame the Data

Don't just push out the data; help the audience understand the data and the message and why it has value for them. As discussed earlier, don't answer a simple question in the here and now, either. Go back in time and create the frame for a clear understanding for your audience.

Your price is data. So is your interest rate or your value proposition. Let's say you're in banking and finance and a potential client asks the question, "What's the interest rate?" If you answer the question simply by stating the rate, the conversation is over. The potential client adds their own frame of reference—by comparing your rate with others they have collected. Who knows where your rate falls among other bank and finance companies.

Instead, here is a simple frame to answer that question that opens, not closes, the door:

Are you asking me for a "quoted rate" or a "locked rate?" There is a big difference. A quoted rate is what the rate is today, and I can offer you basically the same rate as everyone else. There aren't many differentiators in this industry when it comes to rate.

Rates change daily and sometimes hourly, so by the time we get to locking in your rate, it will be different from what it is today. I want to be sure I can fulfill the promise I make to you. That's what's most important to me.

As I mentioned, a "locked" rate is the one that will be on your mortgage and determines your payment. For us to get to that rate, we need to answer a few questions, check your credit, and ensure we choose a loan program that fits your financial goals.

May I ask you a few questions?

This frame or script brings out the fact that there is much more involved in the process than a rate. It also sets you apart as an expert because you educated your audience in the process. In other words, you are framing the message and helping the audience better understand the data. And don't forget that everything in the script is 100 percent true. Proper framing should help customers better understand what they are buying by simplifying the complexities involved.

Before answering a question or approaching a topic, think about the following:

- What is the question you hope to answer, the question behind the initial question?
- Does your answer go back to the past to draw a frame of the why?
- Is your answer memorable?

Address Fear through Frames

As we discussed earlier, the sequence of your presentation matters. Think in terms of the three Ps—predict, preempt, prevent. Often the tendency is for the presenter to ignore the fear of their audience. That's the opposite of the AMPLIFII approach. Just stating the message forces the potential client to fill in the frame, potentially leading them to decide against working with you.

Before ever delivering the message, address the fear, preempt the risks before they come up in thought or discussion. It's about creating safety for the listener—opening their mind to the message. Reframe the negative and take a deeper look.

For example, let's talk about what happens when a new manager takes on a new team. Predictably, the team most likely doesn't know or trust the new manager yet. So rather than immediately describing vision and change—both topics that can trigger defensive mechanisms—the new manager should begin by building relationships and trust.

Perhaps the manager can do that by sharing the personal journey that led them to this position:

> I remember when I first entered this industry as a front-line operator. I was frustrated with my manager because I had so many ideas as to how I felt the business could improve, but they would never listen.

This type of frame or story humanizes the manager and creates a connection through a previous struggle that the team may have shared or is currently undergoing. It shows empathy and emotional intelligence. With more detail, the story could demonstrate that the manager understands their position without having to say, "I understand your position."

Important Message!

- **All the examples in these pages assume that the stories and frames we use are true.**
- **DO NOT make up or lie about a story or frame.**
  - **That's unethical.**
  - **That's wrong.**
  - **That destroys ethos and the ability to earn trust.**

When the time is right, this kind of a frame also tees up a good opportunity to introduce a possible new vision based on the manager's past experience. And it relates well to their current audience.

The best communicators and leaders don't ignore the risks or negative information. They prepare their audiences for them, and they address them head on so they can move past them. Preemptive action is how great athletes approach a game. They study the opposing team's or player's situation and performance; they figure out how it relates to them and the right course of action to take. Then on game day they execute their plan. Such preparation reduces uncertainty (a cause of stress) and allows for peak performance.

Experts do the same thing. When we approach a message knowing that it may cause fear or stress in our audience, we can get ahead of the situation and address it before the audience brings it up. The result is a greater chance of influence.

What Frame Prevails

As mentioned, every conversation, discussion, presentation, interaction, and speech is a battle for attention or meaning. That's the case whether you're negotiating for a better price, participating on a panel, speaking to a group, pitching a product, or simply talking to a friend.

It comes down to understanding whose meaning, whose frame of reference prevails.

The Role of Ethos

That's where your ethos comes into play. If you have the title "Dr." in front of your name, that gives you ethos, credibility, and is part of your brand affecting how others see, hear, and perceive you. The same applies with other titles such as esquire, sergeant, captain, president, or representative. If someone learns about you from an article you wrote, a speech you presented, or even the mention of your name in a video or online, those frames contribute to solidifying your ethos.

Conversely, if you've been recently disparaged on social media or became overly intoxicated at a company gathering, that hurts your ethos and sets you up in a negative frame. Either way, framing follows you. When we start to become comfortable with framing, we start to see it everywhere.

Framing in the Media

One of the most striking places to compare and contrast framing is in the media. It's fascinating to see how the same current event plays differently among various media outlets.

I did a random, unscientific social experiment that basically compared how two different news organizations—FOX and CNN—framed the same story differently. I posted both articles side by side with no comment, commentary, or bias, and waited.

When I checked back, the emotional responses—from hateful to offensive—that the post generated were amazing. It elicited anger and other emotions from all kinds of people and serves as a reminder of the power of framing. Framing something improperly can trigger emotions that work against us. But when something is framed properly, we can actually trigger the emotions that move an idea, message, or relationship forward.

In this instance two broadcast outlets didn't tell us what to think, but they did frame the message of what to think about and created the conversation as a result.

Your Origin Story

A very powerful framing device is your origin story. It answers two big questions—how you arrived at where you are today and why you love serving the customers you serve. This is the frame that draws in your audience, creates credibility, and builds trust. It does not, however, build influence. That comes later.

The origin story—the frame—sets the context for you to deliver your value proposition or core message. If delivered effectively, the message sets the stage for influence.

Uncovering your origin story isn't always easy. Most people seldom reflect on how they got to where they are today or the defining moments early in life that shaped their values. That is where self-awareness can help. Leaders connect because they are aware of their own story, they know where they came from, and they pay attention to the details, including who was and wasn't part of the story. That's how to capture your audience's attention in our busy and crowded world.

When Janice got the frame right the second time around, she set the stage, provided the background, and created the emotional connection or movement with her audience that enabled her to deliver her powerful message. Without the frame, we're left with, "Who cares?" or "So what?" or worse, the wrong frame.

Powerful Takeaways

- Frames are constructs of reality that provide psychological context to help us understand our world. The more common term is *frame of reference*.
- The battle for attention, influence, and even financial resources is a matter of whose frame is perceived as the most credible, compelling, and valuable. Because framing is a collection of concepts, metaphors, and theoretical references that together help us understand reality, story becomes a powerful device to control the narrative.
- Our perceptions of political parties, different ethnicities, the opposite sex, new technology, or a change in strategic direction are all affected by the frames through which we view them.
- Don't just push out data. Frame it. Help the audience understand the data and the message and why it has value for them.
- Framing is everywhere.
- *Do not* make up or lie about a story or frame. It's unethical, wrong, and destroys your ethos and the ability to earn trust.
- Your origin story is a powerful frame. It answers two questions—how you arrived at where you are today and why you love serving the customers you serve.

6

Frames in Action

"A well-thought-out and well-constructed frame is a strategic advantage."

—René Rodriguez

FOR CENTURIES, STORIES have proven to be a powerful way to convey a message. We focus on origin stories as a strong basis for framing. But there are many other frames and types of framing devices.

Props, jokes, quotes, statistics, memes, third-person stories, and even the music you choose to play in a video or as background all influence the experience. The background music in a pricey, upscale restaurant generally is more mellow and soothing than in a casino or bar where it's loud and energetic.

Let's assume that your product is top-of-the-line quality and as a result, more expensive than the competition's. Using the three Ps—predict, preempt, prevent—we can predict that price will come up as a question or objection at some point unless the seller "claims the frame" and preempts or prevents that response.

The influence objective is to shift the frame and conversation away from price and over to quality.

The Alan Shepard Story

A great historical frame involves an interview with astronaut Alan Shepard, the first American to launch into space on May 15, 1961. Imagine the excitement and attention of the moment as the world watched. Also imagine Shepard's fear as he was literally sitting atop a giant hunk of metal to be launched into space with a massive explosion.

Price versus Quality

With the world watching, a reporter had the chance to ask Shepard what was going through his mind before he entered the Mercury space capsule.

He was about to be the first American to launch into space, and the world wanted to know.

Shepard's answer was a classic argument for quality. (Admittedly, there is some confusion as to which early astronaut really said the words, but the context is clear):

> It is a very sobering feeling to . . . realize that one's safety factor was determined by the lowest bidder on a government contract.[1]

Shepard's response was powerful because it was an insight into the age-old argument of short-term versus long-term thinking. I refer to it as the "moment of purchase" mindset (or frame) versus the "time of performance" mindset (frame). At that momentous time in history, all Shepard could think about was that every part on the rocket that would propel him into space was built by the lowest bidder.

Shift From Cost to Quality

The astronaut's statement also was a shift in frame—from monumental excitement and glory to true concern about quality. It certainly grabbed the attention and the emotions of listeners.

This category frame shift serves as a powerful way to influence someone's actions. When one category of frame is perceived as less desirable than another, it often serves as impetus for people to buy into the alternative. In Shepard's case, it was a shift from lowest price frame to the absolute need for highest quality.

Application in Business

The final stages of consumer product purchasing involve two categories. The first is the moment of purchase when the consumer thinks about the importance of the lowest cost and saving money. It's momentary and passes quickly.

The second category is known as time of performance and is more long-lasting. Setting atop the Redstone Rocket aboard the Freedom capsule, astronaut Shepard wasn't thinking about the lowest price in any good way. He was concerned about quality and performance.[2]

Our job as sales professionals, communicators, and leaders is to help people move beyond that short-term moment of purchase thinking into a broader view. Most of the solutions people offer require a "time of performance" mindset to comprehend the value proposition.

In real estate sales, for example, a new agent typically charges the same commission as a seasoned professional. That seems completely illogical because the seasoned pro should be able to offer more value, right? Yes, but only if the seasoned professional can communicate the incremental value. A speaker negotiating a fee faces a similar challenge of negotiating value as opposed to rock-bottom price.

In both situations, a category frame shift can influence the outcome. The story helps the audience move away from the moment of purchase—the short-term thinking—to the bigger picture that focuses on quality and performance.

Client Framing

Clients try to frame or reframe sales professionals all the time. The attempt at reframing usually comes in the form of slow response times to messages—indicating a lack of interest—or comments that someone else can do the same thing cheaper, faster, and easier. The sales professional needs to be able to assess when this happens to avoid the abyss of price reductions, discounts, and concessions.

A well-thought-out and well-constructed frame is a strategic advantage in the marketplace and can pay off handsomely in the long run. In this battle of whose frame will win, a sales professional should be able to understand the viewpoint of their potential client. But the professional also must have a strong belief in their value and be able to communicate it with conviction through metaphor, story, props, and examples. That's how to win the battle of frames.

Historical Frames

The astronaut story is a great way to frame a point. It's a critical and powerful story that evokes emotion, patriotism, and the unexpected. That's why exploring and understanding history can make stories more exciting, interesting, and evocative.

Historical frames don't have to refer to years long past, either. Back to the client considering buying real estate and asking about interest rates. Creating an historical frame can be a solid way to set the stage and address the negative while further establishing your pathos. Sequencing comes into play here too. The conversation with a potential mortgagee might start something like this:

> *I'm so excited that we get to work together. I know you have plenty of options on who to work with, and it means a lot to us that you are here.*
>
> *Before we get started, I know there is a lot of confusion in the marketplace right now and, for some people, fear. The media is having a field day with misinformation, and it's crazy to see how many people buy into it.*
>
> *Unfortunately, the media is not a public service organization. So let's look a little deeper.*
>
> *Many people out there are making money in real estate right now. There are great opportunities to buy real estate if it's done properly and you have the right tools and information.*
>
> *Let me show you what your financial future could look like in five to ten years if you decide to buy this home . . .*

Building Your Frame

Again, think in terms of the three Ps—predict, preempt, prevent—when building your frame. Simply stating the message prompts the potential client to fill in the frame based on their past experiences. And we have no clue if those experiences are positive or negative. Instead, we need to provide the frame to avoid any negative emotional response triggered by a potentially negative frame.

In the conversation with the potential homebuyer, above, the influencer predicted the fear in the market, then preempted and prevented it with a frame from history and the media, and revealed the statistics showing that real estate done properly can be profitable. A true pro would then close the deal with logos (logic) by showing the charts and graphs to build psychological safety (structure, order, and predictability).

The sales rep used keywords, phrases, and concepts to further engage the listener and encourage connection. Concepts such as sharing a secret, pointing to lots of great opportunities, highlighting the benefits for your customer and their family, why, and how are all important, too. The rep literally built a shared connection with his words—his frame—and his delivery. As he spoke, he leaned into his audience.

It is important to remember that in this scenario and with most consumers you can often use phrases such as "opportunity" or "secret." But when dealing with a savvy investor or more sophisticated buyer such as in a corporate purchasing department, words with any remote connection to slick, get-rich-quick schemes will leave you dead in the water. This is a lesson in kairos—you need to know your audience and their world.

Practice the Frame Game

Frames are everywhere. As with anything else, the more we practice creating frames—real or imagined—the better we can become at sharing our stories with maximum impact. A great way to do that is the frame game. It's a game anyone can play anytime and almost anyplace. All it takes is three random objects and a little creativity.

Don't overthink it or stress about the game, either. This exercise is designed to help your reticular activating system (RAS) start to see possible frames in everyday life. This is done best in a team meeting where the audience is committed to learning. You can do this alone, but for best results try it with at least one other person.

The frame game is a staple at AMPLIFII training events. So let's get started.

Enjoy

Step 1: Pick three random objects. Anything is fine—off the desk, on the shelf, from the kitchen; it doesn't matter. Or, as I like to do, ask your kids to choose the objects. This will be your **frame.**

Step 2: Pick three random historical events and write each down on a separate card or piece of paper. This will be your **message.**

Step 3: Choose three lesson topics of interest and write each down on another separate card or piece of paper. Sample ideas: Leadership, why you should prospect every day, the importance of brushing your teeth, or why someone should buy your product or work for your company. This will be your **tie-down.**

The Challenge

You now should have three groups in front of you—one for props, one for current events, and one for lessons. Next, pick one of the objects, one of the cards with an historical event, and one of the cards with a lesson. Are you beginning to realize your task? It's frame time.

Your job is to give a one- to two-minute mini-talk using all three prompts. The object becomes the frame that transitions to the historical event, which then transitions to the tie-down or lesson. It's frame, message, tie-down—the AMPLI-FII formula.

Don't overthink the process of using all three. Your task is to create a viable and complete story arc that makes sense. Most importantly, have fun with the process. If possible, record the session. It makes a great feedback tool for continual improvement.

The Props

My kids brought me three random objects—a Rubik's cube, a graphing calculator, and a small plastic race car.

To refresh your memory, a Rubik's cube is a six-sided three-dimensional puzzle. Each of the usually colorful sides has nine stickers or squares that can be turned over manually. The object of the puzzle is to turn over all the squares so that each side is all the same color.

Also, as a refresher for those of us out of school a long time, a graphing calculator is a large, battery-powered, handheld complex device with rows of buttons and the ability to perform lots of different calculations.

My kids also wrote three lessons they would like to learn more about on the cards—staying healthy, leadership, and honesty. And they wrote down three historical events—Martin Luther King's "I Have a Dream" speech, Space X's recent first launch of private citizens into space, and the COVID-19 quarantine.

Quite an interesting mix of objects and ideas. But it's manageable. After all, this isn't a rigged game. It's spontaneous, and there's no right or wrong answer. There is no perfect message, either—just choose the first one that comes to mind. Remember, the game is about learning how to think quickly and easily, pivot if necessary, and still deliver a compelling message.

Example 1   Rubik's cube, Space X launch, staying healthy

Frame: Rubik's cube
Current event: Space X launch
Tie-down: Maintaining good health

I remember seeing my first Rubik's cube as a child. From a visual standpoint, I loved all its bright colors. And from the puzzle standpoint, I was always fascinated with trying to figure out the strategy to match all the colors on each side.

Beyond that, I also was intrigued by how everything worked inside the cube and how the mechanism enabled someone to keep turning over the little squares. Once I actually even took the entire cube apart just to study the inside.

I really enjoyed taking the Rubik's cube—something so seemingly impossible to decipher—and finding the solution.

(Transition)

I like doing the same thing in life, too. It reminds me of what just happened with the first private Space X passenger launch into space.

A private citizen, Elon Musk, accepted a seemingly insurmountable challenge of figuring out how to develop and build manned space launch capabilities. And now we've just watched not only Elon Musk and his Space X but also Amazon's Jeff Bezos and his Blue Origin take to space—all without government aid or intervention. I think about the complexity of making all that happen.

(Transition to tie-down)

Closer to home, I know many of us struggle to maintain good health, especially with COVID-19 so much a part of our lives over the last months. Staying healthy sometimes can feel as seemingly impossible a goal as privately sending people into space or even solving a Rubik's cube. But there's a strategy; we just have to recognize it, study it, practice it, and make it happen.

When you see someone like Elon Musk or Jeff Bezos achieve the impossible, then it becomes a bit easier to realize that we each can achieve what seems like impossible goals. Health is one of those.

Sound a bit far-fetched? Maybe, but maybe not. After all this is a game to help you become more creative and train your brain to start seeing connections between objects that your audience already understands. Then, as a storyteller, you can leverage those connections to make your message easier to digest.

Taking random objects and ideas and turning them into frame, message, and tie-down is also a skill in improvisation. Its application in business is known as "thinking on your feet." We all get thrown curve balls, and our ability to keep a cool head and reframe situations using our available resources can make or break a deal. The good news is that this is a skill we all can learn.

Look at the frame and the message above. The frame is the cube, the message is the SpaceX launch, and the tie-down is good health. With the frame and the message your audience doesn't know where you're going until the tie-down. That way they don't jump ahead and fill in their own frames and conclusions, and so they remain open to your message and tie-down.

Mastering Transitions

To put together this three-piece puzzle of seemingly unrelated things, we work backward. Look at the tie-down—maintaining good health. Then ask yourself how you can link that in story form to the SpaceX launch and Rubik's cube. What are the common denominators?

The process is called transitioning and is an important skill to learn. When we learn how to transition well, our talks feel seamless and smooth. Good transitions also foster trust because our audience feels that we've done our homework. Our ethos grows, too, because we literally are customizing our messaging to the audience in real time. Customization, remember, is a powerful influencer.

If I know that my story must end with the goal of good health—the tie-down—my thought process begins with: What's the first thing that comes to mind with a Rubik's cube? It's a complex puzzle that's seemingly unsolvable. Isn't that what we all assumed with private space travel, too? No one could possibly develop, let alone afford, the complex technology.

Once you've established that link, then as the storyteller you build the bridge—show the connection to the tie-down.

Are you beginning to understand how to create frames? Try making up another story involving the same challenge.

Example 2   Graphing calculator, COVID-19 lockdown, and leadership

Frame: Graphing calculator
Current event: COVID-19 lockdown
Tie-down: leadership

Remember, it's not about the best story. It's the first story that works, that engages the audience, and conveys the message.
Some ways to approach the challenge:

- What's the tie-down? Leadership.
- What is or are the common denominators in all three prompts? Perhaps the restrictions and fear around a complex problem like the lockdown or leadership.
- Again, let's start the story by setting the frame in the past.

The Frame: *When I was a child in Minnesota, I remember all the smart kids walking around school with these big,*

(Continued)

(Continued)

complex calculators. I never had one because I wasn't in a class that required them. In truth, I wasn't smart enough to be in those classes.

A friend had one, though, and I remember looking at it and getting so confused and embarrassed because I didn't know how to use it. I was scared that if my friend noticed, it would give away that I wasn't smart enough to be in those classes.

The Current Event: *My experience of feeling overwhelmed with the calculator and the fear it caused reminds me of the problems caused by the complexities of the COVID-19 lockdown that we all have experienced at times over the past months, now stretching into years.*

We find ourselves struggling just to make sense of it all, the positive and negative messages. People on one side believing one thing and on the other side saying the opposite. There's no way around it; this is a complex time, especially its effects on the markets, housing, education, our emotional stability, and more.

The Lesson: *Right now is a time when, more than anything else, we need leadership to step up, guide, and help us focus on what we need to do to pull us out of this pandemic-prompted slump. We need leaders to guide us forward and step-by-step so we can build anew. That's whether we're rebuilding our lives, our relationships, or our businesses.*

There's the story—the frame, the message, and the tie-down. We began with three seemingly disparate things. But when we bridge them together with clear transitions, they sound strong and cohesive rather than random.

**Example 3   Race Car, Martin Luther King Jr
Speech, Honesty**

Do you see any similarities among each of these three things?
Before reading on, try building your own frame, message,
and tie-down from the three concepts. Then compare your
story to mine below.

Building the frame isn't that hard. In fact, it can be fun
and challenging. It's satisfying, too, to know that you can
do this. And the more you practice finding similarities and
conveying messages among seemingly unrelated things, the
better you become at conveying your real-life messages.
That's a promise.

The Frame and the Thought Process

*The small race car reminds me of a movie I saw recently, Ford v.
Ferrari. It's the story of how American automotive designer Carroll
Shelby and British race car driver Ken Miles, against all odds and
interference, built a revolutionary new car for Ford. And then how
they challenged Enzo Ferrari at the 24 Hours of Le Mans.*

Shelby's legacy and his engines stand strong as a model today,
too. Despite fierce opposition, Shelby stood up for what he knew
was right and would work, and he succeeded.

Stories of people standing up against opposition always seem
to inspire us, just as civil rights leader Martin Luther King Jr,
who wasn't afraid to go against the system, to stand up for what
he believed in and strive for change. One of his most famous
speeches, "I Have a Dream," stands today as testament to what
he believed in.

King's quest, Shelby's too, to stand up for truth and what they believed in are symbols of the importance of standing up for what we believe—for honesty and truth—no matter the obstacles or the challenges.

It's Your Turn

Now it's your turn to play the frame game. Wander around your surroundings and find three separate and unrelated items. Then take each item and weave a convincing story pairing it as the object with one of the three lessons and one of the historical events.

Or, if you feel particularly empowered, create your own events and lessons, and build your stories from there. Such is the positive power of framing when you are trained to see frames everywhere. Thank you, reticular activating system (RAS).

Powerful Takeaways

- Props, jokes, quotes, statistics, memes, third-person stories, and even music all influence the audience experience.
- A category frame shift can help an audience move away from the moment of purchase—the short-term thinking—to the bigger picture that focuses on quality and performance.
- When building a frame, think in terms of the three Ps—predict, preempt, prevent. When someone simply states the message, that prompts the potential client to fill in the frame based on their past experiences.
- The frame game can help each of us become better at quick thinking, something that pays dividends in business.

7

Messages, Concepts, and Value Propositions

"There are no victims in good communication."

—René Rodriguez

WHEN PEOPLE THINK about communicating, they usually mean the message to be delivered. We as communicators and leaders do everything from overthinking how to deliver the message to not thinking about it enough.

Remember Janice in her mock interview and her proudest moment? Initially she failed to provide a frame. As a result, her message was lost along with any value she could bring to an organization. When she added her frame and tie-down, she connected the dots for the interviewer and clearly conveyed her message—that she can overcome seemingly insurmountable obstacles in life. That was the message she wanted to communicate to her audience.

And, with the addition of her tie-down, we learned she will do the same in business. The tie-down makes sure that the message and lesson are heard clearly in a way that means something to the audience. More on that later.

What Is Your Message?

Most people don't put much thought into the message they are trying to communicate. They just talk, assuming the audience will figure it out. They feel like they understand their message. They have an intuitive sense of what they want, but articulating it isn't so easy.

That's why copywriters are such a valuable asset. They have the ability to listen between so many lines and to find the hidden wants and needs—those unspoken agendas that, if not articulated, lead to inevitable disappointments.

A good message is clear enough for the listener to understand the actions expected of them. The goal is to eliminate as much as possible the need for any assumptions. As is usually said in my profession, "Assume nothing, communicate everything." It's a wise approach when creating a message.

Different Types of Messages

There are all kinds of messages. The AMPLIFII formula facilitates the ability to communicate difficult messages that our brains' defense mechanism might block or the listener misunderstand through lack of the right frame.

Consider some possible messages that might need to be communicated:

- Value propositions;
- Concepts;
- Key messages;
- Mission statements;
- Differentiators;
- Your purpose (your why);
- Innovative ideas;

- Action items;
- Needed changes;
- Expectations;
- Disagreements;
- Difficult truths;
- Feelings;
- Answers to easy or tough questions.

Some of these messages are more easily accepted than others. But all of them risk being misunderstood and can cost time, energy, relationships, and money. The frame in which they're presented, though, will determine how they are received. In essence, the message often helps determine the best frame.

Key Messages

Key messages are the main points of information someone wants their audience to hear, understand, and remember. These are consumable summaries that communicate what you do, why you do it, how you are different, and what value you bring to the table. Key messages clarify meaning and make it easy to remember what you said because it was simple.

From an organizational perspective, key messages are the core of branding and marketing and should be represented in all communications. When people are clear on key messages, what is said can change but the key message doesn't.

Key messages allow for personal expression and creativity in delivery, which promotes authentic communications. Other valuable aspects include the ability to prioritize strategic efforts and define targets. They ensure consistency and accuracy, which are important, especially when rules and regulations compliance is involved. In dealings with the media, they allow a cohesive and consistent message in the face of difficult questioning.

Tips to Create Effective Messages

- Split Messages by Topic
  - A goal could be three to five messages per area of focus. That way the messages are easy to remember, and a design and social media team can easily stay on message.
- Focus on Value
  - The message should illustrate the differentiated value to the intended customer. The more focused and niched the message, the better. Niche messages have more impact and better conversion rates.
- Focus on Action
  - The message should compel an audience to act, so be clear on simple action steps. Anything too complex creates friction, and friction kills conversion.
- Keep It Simple
  - Don't make an audience do any extra thinking. Value should be immediately apparent and memorable. If an audience has to calculate or derive value, then rework the message until it is immediately obvious. This is not as easy as it sounds, but it's worth the effort.
- Tailor Your Message
  - When possible, adjust the message to meet the specific needs of a customer. Anytime we can customize for a customer, we do. In today's noisy world, an ounce of customization goes a long way.

What Makes a Good Message?

Not all messages are created equal. In a world where we are constantly bombarded with demands on our attention, we are required to improve at this ancient skill.

Many messages lack clarity, structure, and purpose. They fail to inform and fill in the gaps of the knowledge needed, and they often are delivered in suboptimal ways.

Messages should persuade. Effective messages provide information necessary to persuade while allowing for collaboration with the target audience. If done correctly, the message is tailored to the specific needs and aptitude of the audience focusing on what is most important and valuable to them.

Choose the right channel. A common mistake is having a great message but delivering it via the wrong channel— sending an email during a heated discussion when you should make a phone call or leaving a voicemail that may never get checked when a text message would likely be read within minutes. One of our clients drafted a paper memo for the entire manufacturing floor outlining new safety procedures. The challenge was 80 percent of the operators didn't speak English and couldn't read.

Video can be powerful under the right circumstances such as wishing someone happy birthday. However, if you were presenting a high-level proposal outlining how special a client is to you, a video might send the wrong message; appearing in person might be the better move. Picking the right channel of communication is crucial to the success of the message.

Be accurate and thorough. I was working with a CEO notorious for responding to emails with short, vague, nonactionable cliches such as "Rock on," "You're a rockstar," and "Boom!" His favorite response was, "You knocked it out of the park!"

As frustrating as his responses were, his intent was to motivate and praise. Unfortunately, he was perceived as lazy in his communication, and he frustrated his people and created confusion, bottlenecks, and uncertainty. When his people needed to know an answer, what was next, or expectations, they would get one of those responses, prompting more phone calls, more attempts at clarifying emails, and possibly poor decisions and job dissatisfaction. Everyone loses with lazy, poor communication.

The Perfect Email

After discussing with my client the effects he was having on his team because of his lazy, ineffective email responses, I shared with him "The Perfect Email," a document I keep on my phone. It was sent to me by the then-head of sales at a multibillion-dollar food company and concerned a keynote I was planning to present to her team.

The email is perfect because it answered *everything* I needed to know for the event. The *who, what, where, when,* and *why.* The author presents all the logistical information, objectives, and company goals, background, opportunities, and next steps. I invite you to take it and keep as a template. Check it out.

The Perfect Email

Rene,

Hope your summer is going well. I wanted to follow up with you about potentially working with the ACME team at our upcoming national sales meeting as follows:

When: Wednesday, October 16 or Thursday, October 17

Where: Radisson Blu

Time: The afternoon of October 16 or anytime on October 17

Background:
The ACME sales team convenes every other year for a national sales meeting. This year is our national sales meeting.

Objectives
- Celebrate FY13
- Align on FY14
- Check YTD results for FY14
- Network
- Continue to learn

Principles
- Feel of a sales meeting
- The customer is our cornerstone
- Keep the messaging simple
- Will be cost conscience

As such, we are spending considerable time and money on pure sales skills this year through a corporate sales effectiveness program. So I feel comfortable that this is a wise investment in core fundamental sales skills.

Opportunity:
When I look at additional skill-building opportunities for the sales and technical sales team, I believe this team can get better in the fundamentals of customer presentations.
As such, I would like to discuss the possibility as follows:

- October 16 (p.m.) would involve two 2.0-hour sessions
- October 17 (a.m. or p.m.) would involve two 1.5-hour sessions
- Attendees: approximately 25 people in each session

(Continued)

Next Steps:
Please let me know:

1. If you are available, and if so, which day and slot (a.m. or p.m.) would you prefer.
2. If you are interested in guiding this type of skill building.
3. The estimated price tag for these services.
4. If needed, how you would like to proceed.

If you would like to set up some time to discuss it, please let me know. You are welcome to schedule something directly with me or via my admin XXXX (555-555-1212).
Look forward to hearing from you.

Thank you,
Sally Best Email Crafter Ever

I know that this sample email seems like a lot to read or even write, but imagine how many phone calls, emails, and time it saved. The executive wrote it one time, and it's done. All that information would be needed regardless, so in reality it took no longer than usual. She just put all the information in one place for people to reference.

Apply the Learning

Use a story to communicate a message. Don't use someone's time to tell them a story.

Janice didn't waste her audience's time with story. Her story was perfectly relevant and carried a message with a clear purpose. A challenge with storytelling is recognizing that the story is not the end goal. It is the means or delivery vehicle for the message. Imagine a gulf between you and your audience that requires a bridge. A good story frame builds that bridge to send your message across.

A Closer Look

For purposes of the AMPLIFII formula, a message is verbal, written, or recorded communication that a listener needs to hear and understand from the presenter's unique perspective. The essential here is *unique perspective*. Each of us views our mission statements, value propositions, feelings, and more from our own perspectives. To have influence, we must not only get others to see things from our perspective but fully understand their perspectives as well. Often, we end up offering our perspective first, and that requires considerable emotional maturity and emotional intelligence.

Messages delivered without a frame risk being misinterpreted because they will be heard through the perspective of the listener. Let's remember the analogy of planting seeds in cement. The seed is your precious message that, if improperly planted, will not take root and die.

I see so many leaders with brilliant ideas quietly waiting to be called on in meetings while the assertive person's half-baked ideas presented confidently and with authority gain support.

That's tragic because the organization misses out on value because leaders don't invite or create the safe space for people to speak up. It's tragic, too, because someone who could have made a valuable contribution on the future of the organization didn't. Instead, they retreated to the familiar.

Planting a Seed/Idea

Frame: *Tilling the soil*
Message: *Planting the seed*
Tie-down: *Watering and nurturing the seed*

Cost of Poor Messaging

With every message, including all of those above, a presenter runs the risk it won't be heard or understood. The consequence of that depends on what is at stake.

With personal messages, if someone in a relationship can't communicate their feelings, they run the risk of creating resentment in the other person. Or, if communicating poorly, they could push a partner away or hurt them.

In business, if someone can't articulate the vision clearly, there's a financial cost. A few of those costs include:

- Productivity losses and delays;
- Leader and worker stress, which can drive up health care costs;
- Distrust that can result in delays in problem solving;
- Disengagement by workers and leaders;
- Poor customer experience because we treat customers the way we're treated at work;
- Employee turnover and associated costs because people leave managers they can't communicate with or don't believe in;
- Creativity and innovation stymied because a brain under stress is not as creative as a calm brain.

Research has shown that the financial cost of miscommunications can be literally tens of millions of dollars per year for some of the biggest companies. One study from Webtorials for Mitel, a global leader in communications, found that the average company loses $11,000 per employee per year in productivity due to poor communications. That same study found that inefficient communication costs the average company with 500 employees more than $5 million a year.[1]

Poor Communication

There's no question, miscommunication is a costly stumble for business. Poorly communicated value propositions lose sales and kill margins by forcing companies into the price-matching game. The same happens with individuals offering services because they end up sounding like a commodity. Miscommunication results in employee disengagement, lack of productivity, and talent loss too.

In fact, in a survey of more than 1,000 people by communications platform Dynamic Signal, nearly two-thirds of employees wanted to quit because ineffective communication interfered with their ability to do their jobs.[2]

Beyond the workplace, poor messaging can cause stress in personal lives. In fact, nearly nine out of ten employees reported that they worry about stress from the workplace.[3,4]

Value Propositions

A value proposition is the *promise* of value that a customer can expect a business, product, or person to deliver. Value is determined in the context of the specific *identified problem* that a business, product, or person solves. A *unique* value proposition is a solution that your competitors can't easily replicate, if at all.

That's a complex definition that we need to break down to better understand how the AMPLIFII formula can help. Let's start with the word *promise*. A promise assumes that the customer believes and trusts you. A powerful story frame can speed up the trust-building process. Add in established ethos (credibility), and you are well on your way.

Identified problem assumes that you have listened and under-stand the unique challenge facing the customer (or market-place). The ability to listen and self-awareness are big advantages in communicating value propositions. The customer may not be aware of the extent of the challenge or the actual cost of not resolving it. Or they may just be in denial.

Last, there are two aspects associated with the word *unique*. The first is whether your product is actually unique or if it is a commodity. If it isn't unique, then the challenge is to show your value is greater, which relies heavily on personal connection, trust building, and relationships. That can be achieved more quickly with personal stories and origin stories as well as other stories that connect with your audience.

If someone is unique but sounds the same as everyone else—uses clichés and the jargon of their competitors—that unique-ness is wasted.

Qualifying the Cliché

I strongly believe that the answers to life can be found in clichés. The first-time a cliché is used, it's not a cliché. It is a powerful truth that communicates a lot with very few words. It's so powerful that people remember it and use it often.

Clichés paint pictures that can sum up lots of words in one phrase. The problem is that no matter how true a cliché, it has very little, if any, impact on an audience because we're desensi-tized to it. It has lost its luster and is no longer novel.

Many of the clichés we use in a business setting aren't the typical "like father, like son" or "an apple doesn't fall very far from the tree." They are overused, weak value propositions that have no impact when used alone. Some examples include:

- World-class service;
- My door is always open;
- Our culture really sets us apart;
- We believe people are our most valuable asset.

All are great ideas but rarely land with impact.

The good news is that using clichés can work with a technique known as *qualifying the cliché*. It's a simple approach that involves adding one phrase immediately before or after the cliché or even in both places. Let's break it down.

Consider the value proposition of world-class service. Alone it doesn't carry impact. But let's qualify it. Before saying the cliché, acknowledge that it's a cliché. For example, take the approach, "I know this sounds cliché, but we offer our clients 'world class service.'" Then immediately follow up with, "Now let me explain what *we* mean by world-class service." And then begin the story.

That approach reflects that the speaker is astute and self-aware. Not acknowledging the cliché detracts from a person's ethos. In telling the story of why yours is world-class service, the speaker stops the audience from creating their own frame of what world-class service is.

Differentiation

Michael E. Porter is one of the world's most influential thinkers on management and competitiveness. He's an author, the Bishop William Lawrence University Professor at Harvard Business School, and director of its Institute for Strategy and Competitiveness. Porter says that there are only three ways to compete or gain a competitive advantage in a marketplace. He defines those three strategy types as cost leadership, differentiation, and market segmentation (or focus).[5]

For our purposes we'll focus on differentiation. Differentiation is often misunderstood as standing out or being different. But it's much more than that. It also is the ability to sell a product or service without having to drop its price.

The best way to understand the role of messaging in the AMPLIFII formula is to examine examples.

The frame tells the story; the value proposition plants the seeds for the message. The latter connects with and opens your audience to listen. The value propositions we have chosen in our work come directly from what we value in our lives. For example, "I chose to work for this company because . . . ."

Delivery, authenticity from the heart, content, messaging, and value proposition all work together to deliver the connection, delivery, and believability. When they're all in sync we achieve the desired result—we're trusted, liked, and known. That's the goal of influence.

When we achieve that harmony, we can deliver our message and wield that influence whether we're nervous or not and even whether we're prepared or not. The essentials are to speak from the heart, exhibit courage, and deliver your message and connect with your audience.

Powerful Takeaways

- A message is verbal, written, or recorded communication that a listener needs to hear and understand from the presenter's unique perspective.
- The AMPLIFII formula facilitates the ability to communicate difficult messages that our brains' defense mechanism might block or the listener misunderstand through lack of the right frame.

- A good message persuades, is delivered via the right channel, and is accurate and thorough.
- Poorly communicated value propositions lose sales and kill margins by forcing companies into the price-matching game. The same happens with individuals offering services because they end up sounding like a commodity. Miscommunications results in employee disengagement, lack of productivity, and talent loss too.
- Using a cliché can work with a technique known as *qualifying the cliché*. It's a simple approach that involves adding one phrase immediately before or after the cliché or even in both places.

8

Tie-Downs: The Master Influencer's Secret Weapon

"Assume nothing; communicate everything."

—René Rodriguez

BECAUSE I HAVE your attention doesn't mean I have influenced you yet. Influence happens through the tie-down.

As we've talked about, communication is complex. There are so many ways a message can get lost from one person to another—in an email, via social media, and even face-to-face. The tie-down is the most powerful way to ensure a message is not only received but also that it is understood exactly as intended.

The tie-down easily cuts through confusion and erroneous or negative frames and locks in the exact message. The tie-down explicitly outlines the precise value of the message in the context of what is important to the audience and their current needs. When you can accomplish all that, the magical outcome is *influence*.

Information Floods Our Brains

Every waking second our brains are flooded with stimuli. We're bombarded with everything from colors, textures, and depths of field to emails, advertisements, sounds, text messages, thoughts, and everything else in our sensory field. The brain must sift through all this and decide what requires attention and what is important.

Making Sense of It All

As we discussed earlier, the brain's first job is to monitor for potential threats. To understand how this relates to tie-downs, let's assume the brain doesn't perceive any potential threats. Once we're safe, the brain now tries to make sense not only of the world around us but also the behaviors of those around us.

With so much information flooding in, the brain must make quick decisions as to what is important and what isn't. That means most information—including your message—in all likelihood could be ignored.

For example, think about how we scroll through and check out social media. With every scroll, we either think, "boring," or "so what," ignore the post and scroll on or we stop for a moment to take a closer look.

This same thought process happens when we speak in person as well. Our audience constantly searches for:

- What this information will mean to them;
- What value it will add to their lives;
- How it will help them achieve their goals.

Context Matters

Context plays a huge role in determining the mindset of an audience. If the audience has paid to attend, they already have decided that there is potential value in the information they are to be provided, so they're receptive to hearing it and taking notes.

Essentially, the influence happened before their arrival. Either marketing, social presence, a book or written article, or a referral of some sort worked in favor of the presenter to prepare the audience (frame them) to see the value in the thoughts and ideas to be presented. These are examples of strategies that grow someone's ethos and make influence and trust happen more quickly.

That's also why it's beneficial to address groups to spread your message among a broader audience. The same kind of influence happens when you create a powerful brand, hire the best photographer to shoot your photos, invest in a compelling website, work with copywriters to flesh out your essence in written word, and engage in social media authentically and strategically.

However, in the absence of these strategies, the right tie-down can create influence. The tie-down is the clearest communication of value to your audience. What makes it so powerful is that it is customized to them specifically. Of course, such customization means you have listened to who your audience is, asked questions, and have empathized with their needs.

Magic Phrase

Again, the tie-down answers the specific question of *what this message means to you,* the audience. That phrase draws a clear connection to exactly what the audience will gain from your message.

Sometimes the tie-down could be simple. Here's an example of a situation with my children when they were younger. My influence objective was to get them to brush their teeth daily.

Pre-framing or the setup.   I called my boys, who were ages four and seven, into my office. They came running in, sat on my lap, and the following conversation ensued:

> *Hey guys, I want to show you something. You know how Daddy goes into the bathroom every morning and before bed to brush his teeth?*
> *Yeah.*
> *Do you know why I do that?*
> *So our teeth stay clean?*
> *Yep. But I am curious; let's do a Google search. (Side note: kids love Google searches.)*

Prop frame—Google images.   The conversation continues. I said:

> *What happens when we don't brush our teeth?*

By now, the boys were looking at Google search images of people with rotten teeth falling out, and the looks on their faces said it all.

The Tie-Down.   I said:

> *It's also so our teeth don't fall out. Do you want your teeth to look like that?*

Still shocked by the photos, they shook their heads. Then I asked them:

> *Do you want to brush your teeth?*

They immediately ran upstairs to do so.

Notice how the conversation and the tie-down weren't elaborate or complex. It didn't need to be because it was tailored to them—the audience—specifically. A powerful image created the emotion I needed and gave them a glimpse into the future. The tie-down (what it means to them) was crystal clear—if you don't brush your teeth daily, your teeth will look like that.

The frame creates the emotional movement, but it needs to be directed at something. Emotion for the sake of emotion in business can be frustrating and uncomfortable. The tie-down allows you to funnel the emotion (pathos) created in the frame laser-like to a specific action. That action is your influence objective (IO).

Influence Objective (IO)

To effectively execute the tie-down, your influence objective—the behavior you hope to influence—must be clear. The influence objective is the specific action, thought, or behavior you are trying to influence. It's easy to see why it can easily be confused with a *call to action*. Again, although there can be overlap, the two are different. Let's consider Janice again. Remember, she was interested in being hired by the mega corporation. Her influence objective (get hired), therefore, drove her tie-down, which I'll present again:

> *If I get the opportunity to work with you, there will be times when we think the challenges are insurmountable and our backs will be against the wall. But know that I'll be right out there working next to you as hard as I can to overcome the challenges in the same way I overcame challenges in my personal life but this time for you and your team.*

What makes this so powerful is that Janice used her frame to explain to her audience why she would make a great hire even though she wasn't asked to do that. She connected emotionally, then tied it all down, and influenced her audience to make her the clear choice. When you have a clear influence objective, the tie-down becomes clearer and easier to identify.

This sounds relatively simple, and it is. But to deliver the messaging effectively requires all the skills of listening, self-awareness, and empathy. A story, statistics, or quotes without a tie-down is like a joke with no punchline. It's unfinished and doesn't add value. For maximum impact, we need to consistently speak in terms of what our messages mean to our audiences. Unfortunately, many people lose sight of that.

The tie-down is not necessarily a call to action although both are closely linked. What makes it especially difficult to get the tie-down right is the assumption that because a message is shared, it is understood. Too often people assume that because they have spoken clearly, their message has been heard. They also assume that the listener can connect all the dots, that listeners know what has been said or presented, and what it means to them. That is a dangerous assumption that often leads to confusion, misunderstanding, or loss of sales.

Assume Nothing, Communicate Everything

One of my memorable college professors shared some profound advice about communication. In all his years of counseling married couples, he said, the best advice he could give to us, his students, was, *assume nothing and communicate everything*.

In other words, he offered us a simple approach to help eliminate the biggest challenge in communication—assumptions.

Grounding the Message

Picture an intended message as a balloon filled with helium. If we simply let it go, it floats away and goes wherever the wind blows. To keep it from floating away, we have to secure it to something—tie it down.

The same is true for your message. If you assume your audience gets it, then it's like letting that balloon go and hoping for the best. It may or may not float in the right direction. The tie-down ensures that your listeners and your audience understand what you are saying and, most important, what it specifically means to them.

Features and Benefits

A fundamental lesson in sales is how to present features and benefits. In our case, we're using features and benefits as the frame to help understand tie-downs. Features are the technical or descriptive aspects of a product, and benefits are the specific ways a product adds value.

Here are some simple examples:

- **Mobile phone:** Feature: facial recognition; benefit: increased security to protect from hackers.
- **Diet soda:** Feature: no sugar added; benefit: no unneeded calories, so weight loss is easier.
- **Tradeshow upgrades:** Feature: floor padding; benefit: reduces fatigue and plantar fasciitis on the bottom of the feet from standing all day.

Hopefully you're beginning to get a clearer picture of the connection and value of tie-downs as they relate to your message. You have read this already, but it's absolutely worth repeating: At a high level, a tie-down is the benefit of your message to the listener. But communicating it is complicated because of the many intangibles of your audience, including ideas and emotions. We also must factor in the audience's or client's specific needs, state of mind, and current situation. That's a lot to digest, but all of it is important.

If you remove the benefits from the equation, you only trigger both Broca's and Wernicke's specific areas of the brain that are responsible for processing language. These two tiny areas of the brain don't contribute to behavior change.[1]

When we return benefits to the equation by means of a tie-down, we trigger the brain to imagine future benefits, draw vivid pictures, and feel the benefits. That anticipation releases the chemical dopamine (the happy hormone) as well, which is positive when we're trying to influence behavior.

Statistics With No Tie-Down

Let's analyze another example, this time with statistics. First, consider the statistics without a tie-down or benefit:

- 97 percent of buyers search for their homes online[2]
- 56.75 percent of all Internet traffic is mobile[3]
- 96 percent of Internet users increased their video consumption in 2020[4]

These statistics without a frame or tie-down force the reader to derive their value, if they derive any value at all.

We see this lack of framing and tie-downs repeatedly in the financial industry where an expert simply shares a statistic. Click on the news to see how much information would be so much more valuable, easier to understand, and more interesting if we as listeners or viewers could understand how it affects us. That includes statistics such as the gross domestic product (GDP), jobless claims, inflation, oil prices, interest rates, and even the Dow Jones Industrial Average (DJIA).

To be fair, some organizations do try to explain the meaning behind the numbers. But those explanations often are generalizations, and without a tie-down they don't convey how they specifically relate to each of us. If your industry uses such information to work with consumers, then your success depends on your ability to use tie-downs with your customers.

Statistics With a Tie-Down

Let's look at those same statistics presented with a tie-down:

- 97 percent of buyers search for their homes online.[5] **Tie-down:** If you are a real estate agent and you don't have an online presence, you risk losing your clients to those who do.
- 56.75 percent of all Internet traffic is mobile.[6] **Tie-down:** If your website isn't mobile-friendly, you are alienating more than half the visitors to your website.
- 96 percent of Internet users increased their video consumption in 2020.[7] **Tie-down:** You need to invest in creating powerful and compelling videos that communicate your value proposition or you will be left in the dust.

The above tie-downs communicate to the reader how the statistics can affect them and what the expected gains or losses might be. The numbers assume greater meaning because we understand their consequences.

Similar information can have a different value to different audiences. It can become even more complex among various people in the same audience, too. That's why it's so important to know your audience and to have enough tie-downs to address the needs of everyone.

Interest Rates Up 0.5%

Now let's look closely at how the tie-down can change, depending on the audience. The statistic in this case is that mortgage interest rates climbed half a point. See how we tie down the data to three different audiences.

- **For a mortgage loan officer**: *What this means to you is . . .*
  - o The number of clients interested in refinancing will slow, so you need to focus on increasing your mortgage purchase business.
- **For a real estate agent**: *What this means to you is . . .*
  - o Your client's buying power will decrease slightly, so you may have to adjust their property search criteria.
- **For the consumer**: *What this means to you is . . .*
  - o This is great news because your interest rate already has been locked by your bank. So relax and enjoy the fact that you secured the best rate possible.
  - o Or:
  - o Because you chose to wait and didn't lock in your loan last week as we discussed, your payment has increased by $47 a month. I highly recommend we lock now to avoid any other unnecessary increases in your monthly payment.

Notice how each tie-down is different. The message offers value to the audience when we understand specifically what that message means for them. The tie-down draws a clear connection between the message and its meaning.

Round and Round the Roundabout

Not providing a tie-down, even for something mundane, is a risk. A change occurs, and we're left to our own frames or lack thereof to decide what it means.

On a trip to Europe as a child, I remember my introduction to the traffic roundabouts at intersections (those are the one-way, circular intersections used in place of traffic lights). A missing tie-down is like being stuck in an endless roundabout.

I was annoyed when they started popping up here in the United States. My only frame of reference was the confusion and annoyance from my trip to Europe. So when they appeared in my city, I applied that frame.

But, had those roundabouts been introduced with a frame and a tie-down, it would have been a completely different story. Not until a few years ago did I come to appreciate their value. Roundabouts are designed to improve safety and efficiency for motorists, bicyclists, and pedestrians.

Some people love them, and some hate them. They annoyed me until I decided to investigate why we use them. The statistics are impressive. The use of roundabouts:

- Reduces fatalities by 90 percent;
- Decreases injury crashes by 76 percent;
- Reduces pedestrian crashes by 30 to 40 percent;
- Increases traffic capacity by 30 to 50 percent.

They are also eco-friendly, reducing fuel consumption and carbon emissions, vehicle delay and the number and duration of stops, compared with signalized intersections. With that frame and tie-down, I don't mind roundabouts anymore. The new frame changed my construct of reality and prompted a completely different experience of them.[8]

When we learn to connect with people through a clear frame, message, and tie-down—the AMPLIFII formula—the listener not only is engaged but influenced.

Entry Ramps

Over the years I have learned that one of the fastest ways to better transition from one part of a presentation/talk/message to another is through the use of *entry ramps*. Entry ramps are simply transition phrases that quickly signal to the audience what is coming next. They help the presenter/speaker stay on track, too.

The easiest and most common entry ramp or transition to the tie-down is: *"The reason I share that with you is . . . ."*

This powerful phrase serves many purposes, but most importantly, it transitions the presenter to the tie-down. This transition phrase signals the listener that the value is about to be delivered.

When we first learn and begin to practice sequence, we often gravitate to that phrase. And that's OK. My good friend and client Tyler Lorenzen, CEO of PURIS Foods, is a master at using the AMPLIFII formula and multiple framing methodologies. One day I received a text message from his wife, Alyssa, saying there had to be more than one way to set up the tie-down and that she was getting tired of hearing, "The reason I share this with you is . . . ."

I laughed. This is common when people first learn about tie-downs. Alyssa then shared that she and Tyler had thought of 20 other entry ramps to avoid sounding repetitive. Here they are:

- What this means to you is . . .
- I share this/that story with you because . . .
- Why this matters to you is . . .
- I believe this matters to you because . . .
- The point of all this is . . .
- This is relevant to you because . . .
- My point is . . .
- I bring this to your attention because . . .
- I invite you to consider . . .
- This is applicable in your situation because . . .
- What's in it for you is . . .
- The reason you should care is . . .
- This is pertinent information because . . .

- The value to you is . . .
- This relates to you because . . .
- The reason that is cool is . . .
- This is significant because . . .
- This directly correlates to you because . . .
- This is very fitting because . . .
- This story is appropriate because . . .

A tie-down should drive the behavior to achieve the objective. With frame, message, and tie-down, there's no question about what I want you to do. I've inspired you with my message. If you have inspired and led people and they have given you the privilege of wanting to follow you, it's your mission to create the path of where to go.

Powerful Takeaways

- The tie-down easily cuts through confusion and erroneous or negative frames and locks in the exact message.
- The tie-down explicitly outlines the precise value of the message in the context of what is important to the audience and their current needs. When you can accomplish all that, the magical outcome is *influence*.
- A story, statistics, or quotes without a tie-down is like a joke with no punchline. It's unfinished and doesn't add value.
- Picture an intended message as a balloon filled with helium. If we simply let it go, it floats away. To keep the message from floating away, we have to secure it to something—a tie-down.
- Tie-downs should be tailored to a specific audience.
- A fast way to better transition from one part of a presentation/ talk/message to another is through the use of *entry ramps*. These are transition phrases that quickly signal to the audience what is coming next and helps the presenter/speaker stay on track, too.

PART

III

The Skills

9

The Art and Science
of Storytelling

*"Potential stories are everywhere if we take the time to listen
and look for them."*

—René Rodriguez

THE DAY WAS August 14, 2003. I was in New York City on the
18th floor of the Liz Claiborne Building giving a presentation to
the vice presidents of the company's apparel division.

This was a big day for me. Liz Claiborne was a new, high-
profile client outside of my typical manufacturing client base, and
all the decision makers were in the room. Everything was going
perfectly; my stories, my timing, and my tie-downs were all on
point. I was even dressed head to toe in Liz Claiborne clothing
that I had purchased the night before just so I could tell the story.

It was three hours and 45 minutes into my four-hour presentation when suddenly the lights got very bright. It reminded me
of what had happened when a fuse had blown out at my house.
Then the power went out!

A power outage usually isn't a big deal. But to put this outage
in context, it happened less than two years after the tragedies of
9/11. We were in Manhattan not far from the site of the World

Trade Center towers that had collapsed. This was long before the United States had tracked down the mastermind of the al-Qaeda terrorist attacks, Osama bin Laden.

Two of the Liz Claiborne vice presidents in my audience started to cry, and panic set in. The president then stood up and left the room to check out what had happened. He returned about three minutes later and said the power was out along the East Coast. That's when we knew things were serious. (This was the 2003 blackout in New York City, which affected 50 million people across eight states and part of Canada. It ended up lasting 29 hours.[1])

The Back Story

I share this story because I had recently finished my first professional speakers' training where I learned the concept of signature stories. In that class, I was surrounded by professionals, CEOs, and others older and much more experienced than I, who undoubtedly had amazing stories to tell. At that moment. I felt I had no stories to tell.

One exercise in my training involved having 12 minutes to create a speech using a signature story, which is a story as unique to each of us as our signatures. (More on that later.) My fellow classmates had told stories of interactions with the CIA and Ku Klux Klan, war, hostile takeovers, and plane crashes.

Then there was me, who had recently finished college. I was racking my brain for a story to tell. With just 4 minutes left of the 12 to write, I approached the instructor practically in tears of stress and told him I couldn't think of anything to share. He looked at me, smiled, and said, "You have three minutes" and then walked away. In the following three minutes I came up with the story of Jesse Arbogast, a young boy whose arm was bitten off by a shark. I used the story to illustrate how money wasn't enough to motivate us to jump into a shark-infested pool. But if our child fell in and was in danger, we dive in without hesitation. That is one of the most powerful stories I have shared in my career.

More important, that exercise taught me that potential stories are everywhere and that we need to watch for them. The instructor also told us we should imagine that each signature story is worth $50,000. So collect those stories and treat them as that valuable.

Suddenly, on that day in New York when the power went out, those thoughts were front and center. I realized I needed to capture every story that happened during this time. So I pulled out my BlackBerry (the handheld device of the time) and started taking notes. I began paying attention to people's reactions, their behaviors, and anything that could possibly contribute to a story.

I noticed who stepped up as a leader and who sat back waiting to be led. Turning my attention to these details reduced my stress and allowed me to think clearly.

The Stairwell

The first story involved 18 of us who made our way to the stairwell and down the stairs in the dark. New York City stairwells have no lights—or at least there were none back then. And in 2003, cell phones didn't have flashlights and their screens weren't bright enough to illuminate the way.

We had to hold hands and make our way down all those flights of stairs. We were doing all of this still thinking that we might be under terrorist attack because no one knew the blackout was caused by human error. All we knew was that the power was out across a of huge swath of the United States. With 9/11 so recent in memory, everyone was on high alert, and many still suffered post-traumatic stress disorder (PTSD).

We finally made it to the ground floor. The array of responses from people on the street ranged from people screaming about the end of the world to others acting as if nothing unusual was happening. It was fascinating, strange, and scary all at the same time.

Jonathan the Bellman

Getting back to my hotel was my priority, so I headed that way. I'll never forget the Hilton Times Square chief bellman, Jonathan, standing at full attention amid the chaos at the front door. Somehow, he spotted me and gave me the biggest smile, grabbing the door and saying, "Welcome back, Mr. Rodriguez. Don't worry we have a generator."

The immediate sense of relief and comfort he provided was priceless. His ability to remain cool, calm, and professional during crisis is very difficult to train and something most organizations only dream of having.

Later that day I learned that Jonathan had a wife and young child in the hospital, but he could not visit because the ferry was shut down. Nonetheless, he remained professional and delivered world-class service to everyone he encountered amid the chaos. I will never forget his discipline and how difficult that must have been for him.

Glow Sticks

As I approached the elevators, a man with a box of glow sticks (or light sticks) blocked the entry. He was checking room keys and then grabbing the glow sticks, opening the package, cracking them to light them up, and then handing them to hotel guests.

This man was frantic and panicked. People were asking him not to turn on the sticks because it was only 2:30 in the afternoon. But in his panic, he couldn't listen and kept repeating that it was policy and there was nothing he could do. The more people yelled at him, the more he resisted.

I stood back and watched and knew exactly what was going on. He was in high-resistance, high-stress mode. I needed to calm him so I could convey the message that he was acting irrationally. But if I took the same approach as everyone else, I would get the same response—defensiveness that only fed his irrationality.

I slowly walked around behind him and began to thank him for being there for us and told him what a great idea it was to have glow sticks. He looked over his shoulder at me somewhat confused and muttered, "Thank you." Then I asked him how long the glow sticks last. He looked back at me, and said, "Huh?" I repeated my question, "How long do those glow sticks last?"

I knew the answer, but posing the question forced him to think differently. He began to slow down as he said, "About four to five hours." I said, "That's amazing" and then asked him the current time. You could see that he was slowing down even more as he handed out the sticks. Then he stopped, looked at me, grabbed a handful of them, and handed them to me uncracked, saying, "Don't tell anybody I gave these to you."

New Skill and Awareness

These are just three of the more than 50 stories I captured during a 48-hour period in New York. I was blown away and excited by this new skill and newfound awareness.

The reality is that stories are everywhere if we learn to look for them. Our reticular activating system (that part of our brain that says, "Yes, listen" or "Forget about it") is designed to discern what is important. When stories become important to us, we will create a category for them in our minds and begin to see them everywhere.

It's like when we buy a new car thinking we're the only ones with this car, and then the moment we drive off the lot, we see the same car everywhere.

Value of Stories

Whenever we kick off AMPLIFII events over dinner, I begin with this story frame. You can take a plain piece of chicken with no story and it ends up on the dollar menu at a fast-food restaurant or take-out shop. Now take that same piece of chicken, build a story around it, the farm it came from, how it was meticulously prepared by a five-star chef, and presented with the utmost attention to detail. Suddenly that $1 piece of chicken is part of a $100 per person tasting menu.

It's the same chicken and the same value proposition, just a different frame. Such is the power of storytelling to completely transform and shift our experience and reality.

Let's face it, we as humans have a tough time resisting a good story, whether it's water cooler gossip, a social media post, a Go Fund Me appeal, a movie, a favorite show, or simply a fun experience.

Narratives and Science

Almost three decades ago I chose to focus my life and career on the application of science rather than the discovery of it. My passion was and still is implementation and application. I was relentlessly curious in my pursuit to try things out. My failures in basketball gave me the gift of resiliency that serves me now.

I share this because it frames an interesting topic—the exactness or literal truth of science versus the metaphorical value of the narrative story we can create to understand and apply the science.

American entrepreneur Jim Rohn said, "While some people are studying the roots, others are picking the fruit."[2]

We need both types of people. Personally, I see myself as the liaison, bridging the gap between both worlds. I was an odd duck in school; I hated math but loved statistics. My mother explained that it was because statistics is a search for truth. That made sense. I also loved science but only when I could see its clear application and value to my life. That was the pragmatic side of me. So when I learned about the science of storytelling, I was immediately captivated. I knew that this would be a lifelong focus. I also knew that I was in for a quiet battle between science and narrative because both attempt to relay truth.

Different Constructs

Some say that storytelling can distort science and contribute to misinformation. We see that every day on social media and in the news and politics as people selectively choose to share what serves their biases. It is also true that storytelling is the most powerful way to engage an audience in complex concepts and ideas. The right story can move audiences to support extremely complex business ventures and give money to finance them.

Very much like framing, science, and storytelling (narrative) represent two different ways to construct reality. Science searches for objective patterns that outline general truths about the world, while narratives outline the connections through the human experience that help us create meaning and value around our reality.

Regardless of their differences, both are essential because they help us make sense of the world and find our place within it.

Efficient Operation

Our brains build models of reality by throwing irrelevant information away. Stories are a natural way our brain organizes the data pouring in daily. Stories allow us to build a simplified model of reality to make sense of the world around us. We don't suffer from brain overload, however, because our brains also function on a use-it-or-lose-it basis.

For example, it's easier to learn a language at a young age because we're born with countless neurons in our brains. The neurons are programmed to understand various sounds associated with different languages. If we don't hear a particular vowel sound, for instance, the brain prunes the neurons designed to hear it for efficiency. This use it or lose it reality is called neural Darwinism. That's why people often have a more difficult time learning a new language later in life.

This pruning process isn't only for sounds. It applies to other stimuli, too. The brain always seeks ways to filter out sensory input that it deems unimportant or not relevant to current needs. To maximize our influence, we must understand how the brain chooses to either retain or filter certain sensory input. Your message depends on understanding this.

Think about it. Our brains are constantly deciding what's valuable and what's not. That's where storytelling becomes a powerful tool. As mentioned earlier, a story becomes the logical and natural way to organize or categorize data into a simplified, usable—what's valuable to me at this moment—model of reality. We love these stories because our brains on some level perceive the storyline to be real. They elicit an emotional response.

Power of the Story

Some research indicates that we humans spend at least a third of our waking hours daydreaming.[3] Other research pegs that number at nearly half—47 percent—of our waking hours. The reason we daydream is that the largest part of our brains, the neocortex, is charged with trying to predict the future to prepare us for various eventualities—what if this happens or that happens. Daydreaming is simply scenario planning or future simulations. That's right, our minds are wandering, and we're thinking about something other than what's in front of us.[4]

And the Brain

Brain scans have shown that when we're caught up in a story, our attention narrows to the present moment. In essence, we stop daydreaming because the storyteller is doing the daydreaming for us. The storyteller is building the narrative inside the listener's mind.

In fact, when someone listens to a story, they aren't just listening, they are fully present. It's the same level of awareness as if they were in a life-and-death situation—as attuned to the message as if someone were pointing a gun at them. That level of acute focus is known as attentional narrowing.

As a communicator, think of the power of the story you weave, the frame you set up to capture your client's or your audience's attention. And consider the power you wield to communicate your message.

The Process

So many different elements are involved in storytelling—from German novelist and playwright Gustav Freytag's dramatic arc to Joseph Campbell's monomyth or hero's journey—a 17-stage path to heroism.[5] It's easy to get caught up in the details and complexities of how to craft the perfect story. But I don't want to do that here; I want to keep this very simple.

Your Story Formula

It has been said that there are only seven basic narrative plots in storytelling that are used repeatedly just swapping out different characters. Those seven types of story, according to *The Seven Basic Plots: Why We Tell Stories* by Christopher Booker (Bloomsbury), are:

1. **Overcoming the monster;**
2. **Rags to riches;**
3. **The quest;**
4. **Voyage and return;**
5. **Rebirth;**
6. **Comedy;**
7. **Tragedy.**

It's important to understand that your story most likely fits into one of those categories, and you need to tell it. Because our brains understand these familiar story lines, we can more easily pay attention and learn from them. It's no different from the reason so much pop music sounds the same. There is a formula.

Just because there's a formula or the story line might be the same, though, doesn't mean the content is similar. It means that we can more easily follow the patterns and structure and our brains don't get distracted. That way it's easier to focus on the message being delivered.

The Heart and the Brain

For the purposes of influence and the ability to have an impact on others, we need to allow our hearts to speak in a sequence that our listeners' brains understand. And for that to happen, we need to gain access to the heart.

Concerning communication, the heart includes three elements—our personal values, beliefs, and memories. We know that our values are formed early in life. Without getting caught up in specific ages, we know that the early years of our lives are formative. They determine in a large part who we are and what captures our attention and our hearts. Those formative years also contribute to determining our focus and our purpose in business.

Stories engage us because of how our brain deals with attention. Our senses interpret a story almost as if it were real. We love movies because our brains perceive those scenes as real, lighting up our sensory cortex like a Christmas tree.

Have you ever cried while reading a book or watching a movie? The characters don't exist. Yet you respond emotionally to what's on the screen or in the pages. Through story, we truly experience what others experience, even if they are fictional.

When we hear a story, our body releases happy hormones, including cortisol, dopamine, and oxytocin.[6] More specifically, cortisol helps us formulate memories, dopamine is involved with emotional responses, and oxytocin is linked to empathy.[7]

The release of oxytocin causes feelings of empathy, and we experience loss, for example, as if it were our loss. We experience victory as if we won the championship. This is an example of how pathos plays a powerful role in influence.

The Science

Beyond the fact that we all enjoy a good yarn, there's science supporting why that is.

Research also has shown that the kind of story we tell affects levels of oxytocin and in turn the level of cooperation of others, according to Paul J. Zak, a professor of economic sciences, psychology, and management in Claremont Graduate University's

Division of Politics and Economics. Zak also was a pioneer in neuroeconomics, the integration of neuroscience and economics.

The amount of oxytocin released by the brain, for example, can predict how much people are willing to help others. Based on additional studies, which included funding from the US Department of Defense, Zak found that when we tell a story that includes tension in the plot, our listeners pay more attention and feel the same emotions conveyed by the story.

For those with doubts about the scientific connection, this transfer of emotions is illustrated by how many people feel dominant after watching a hero or superhero movie—like James Bond, 007, saving the world or Marvel's Avengers defeating evil.

"When you want to motivate, persuade, or be remembered, start with a story of human struggle and eventual triumph. It will capture people's hearts—by first attracting their brains," says Zak.[8]

Zak relates the neurobiology of storytelling to business with the following:

"My experiments show that character-driven stories with emotional content result in a better understanding of the key points a speaker wishes to make and enable better recall of these points weeks later."[9]

Therefore, the story—the frame—becomes one of the most powerful ways to connect with your audience. When you tell a story, your audience becomes so engrossed in the narrative that they place themselves in the story.

Empathy

Story also is one of those few ways humans can truly experience another's perspective. That's real empathy. We do that not only by telling stories but also by listening to our clients' stories, too.

One study found that after listening to a good story for two weeks, the listeners actually reported the ideas in the story as their own. That study appeared in *Applied Cognitive Psychology*, a peer-reviewed journal.[10]

This degree of acceptance is why branding agencies and political campaigns spend billions of dollars on building powerful, emotional narratives that move people. These professionals know that the stories will be adopted at a deep level and then defended as one's own. The results are purchases and votes.

The Trust Factor

In telling stories, we make our way into the listeners' brains and can create the desired narrative *if*, and that's a big if, there is trust. If trust is established, stories actually can influence how people think and make decisions.

The best salespeople, leaders, and organizers create great narratives and powerful stories that deliver a message to help others take action. They understand the power of what they say and how they say it.

Try the following exercise to help you identify those values that matter to you.

The Warning

Storytelling is a tool of influence that can be misused, too. Organizers often use story to incite crowds to protest or riot. Villains can have strong frames that generate hate, racism, and violence.

With the power of influence, it's important to remember that a story is like a gun or a car. It can be used for good or evil. The work we do, I believe, is sacred because our work—this

MY VALUES

Sometimes life can be stressful and it is during those times that we need something powerful to drive us.

Motivation wears off quickly, but our values, when aligned with our actions, can be the most powerful driver of all.

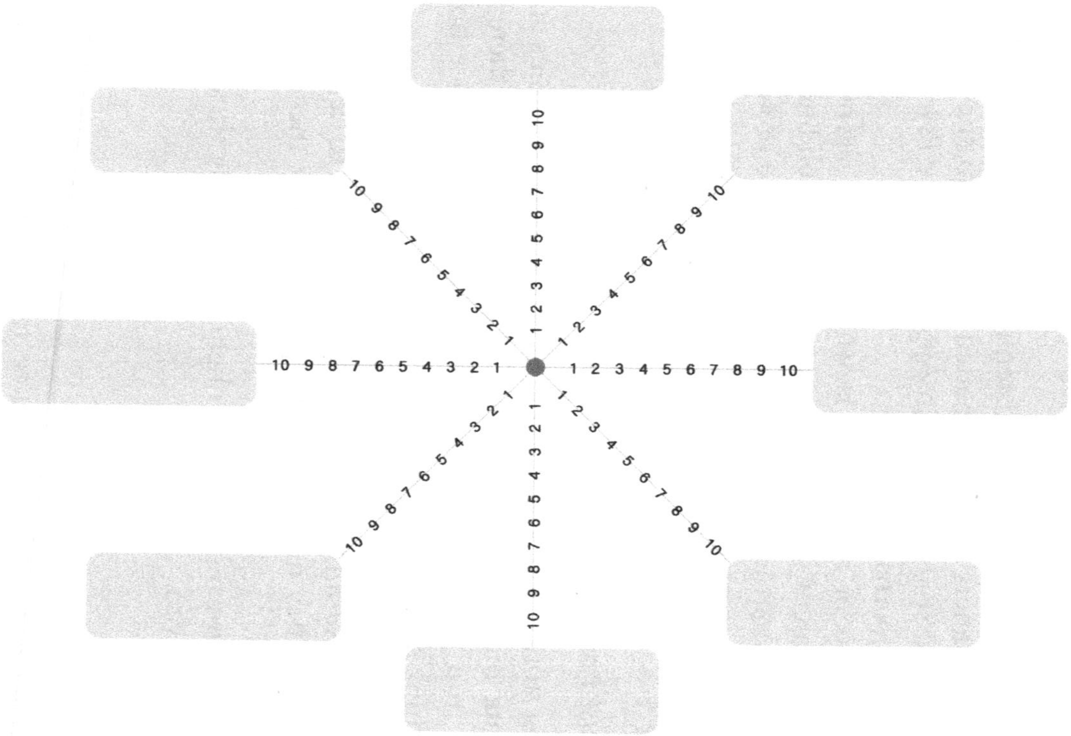

Figure 9.1

MY VALUES

(continued)

Instructions:

1. Circle 8 guiding values in the list and then write those values in the empty boxes below.

2. Rate each value by circling the number—10 being the highest, as to how well you feel that you are living that value.

3. Connect the dots to see where you might be off balance.

4. Adjust your life to integrate more balance. How does your wheel look?

Acceptance	Discretion	Inspiration
Accountability	Diversity	Integrity
Achievement	Eagerness	Intelligence
Adventure	Education	Intensity
Affection	Effectiveness	Intimacy
Appreciation	Efficiency	Joy
Assertiveness	Empathy	Justice
Balance	Encouragement	Kindness
Boldness	Enthusiasm	Leadership
Bravery	Excellence	Learning
Candor	Faith	Love
Caring	Family	Loyalty
Challenge	Fidelity	Motivation
Change	Flexibility	Openness
Cheerfulness	Forgiveness	Optimism
Clarity	Freedom	Organization
Collaboration	Fun	Passion
Commitment	Generosity	Perseverence
Communication	Grace	Power
Compassion	Gratitude	Punctuality
Community	Growth	Quality
Confidence	Happiness	Relationships
Consistency	Harmony	Resourcefulness
Contribution	Hard Work	Respect
Control	Health	Security
Courage	Honesty	Service
Creativity	Humility	Teamwork
Decisiveness	Independence	Trust
Dependability	Influence	Unity
Determination	Innovation	Wisdom

Figure 9.1 (*Continued*)

MY STORY MATRIX

I BELIEVE			
I REMEMBER when			
I was TAUGHT			
I am PASSIONATE about			

Figure 9.2

influence—changes the world, creates the environment in which we live and the communities we serve, and affects our homes and our children. If you want to affect the world, do good work, and move people. Learn to tell your story.

Powerful Takeaways

- Stories are a natural way our brain organizes the data pouring in daily.
- Stories allow us to build a simplified model of reality to make sense of the world around us.
- There are only seven basic narrative plots in storytelling that are used repeatedly just swapping out different characters.
- Our brains constantly decide what's valuable and what's not. That's where storytelling becomes a powerful tool.
- We love these stories because they elicit an emotional response.
- When someone listens to a story, they are fully present. It's the same level of awareness as if they were in a life-and-death situation.
- Stories engage us because of how our brain deals with attention. Our senses interpret a story as if it were almost real.
- If trust is established, stories can influence how people think and make decisions.

10

Body Language and Presence

"The average person looks without seeing, listens without hearing, touches without feeling, moves without physical awareness . . . and talks without thinking."
—*Leonardo da Vinci*[1]

YOUR BODY INTRODUCES you before your words. More than ever before, today people make snap judgments based on first impressions. That's why body language is central to the influence tool set.

The same holds true for nonverbal cues such as tone of voice, eye contact, inflection, and how close we stand to someone. Those cues all convey specific messages that affect our influence.

To understand the cues you give and receive requires self-awareness, mindfulness, humility, empathy, emotional intelligence, and discipline—the basic skills of leadership and influence. The good news is that those skills can advance people in most industries as well as personal relationships. Body language can be the guide that offers subtle clues if we learn to listen without agenda or ego.

The Work Begins Inside You

There are tools, techniques, and even some secrets of successful body language. But the reality is that when we speak with authenticity and passion, our bodies know exactly what to do and how to be congruent with our words.

In these pages you will learn how to align your body with the natural authentic movement of a message that is congruent with the words spoken from the heart.

Micro-Expressions

A CEO of a large bank was frustrated with his leadership team because he didn't think they took him or his vision seriously. He brought me in to help him prepare to deliver another message to the team.

We set up a camera, and he gave his speech so I could study his delivery. As he began to talk, I noticed something interesting around his face, specifically his mouth. At first, I wasn't sure what it was, but then it happened repeatedly, and invariably when he discussed a certain idea. I zoomed the camera in to his mouth and kept recording.

I also noticed that whenever he talked about financial projections, he sniffled and slightly cleared his throat. When we played back the video frame by frame to watch the micro-expressions, we saw what was happening. It was so quick that the eye had a hard time seeing it. But I guarantee you the amygdala (remember, that's the part of the brain that monitors sensory inputs for signs of threat) could pick it up. Whenever he talked about the numbers and sniffled, we paused the playback. And every time he was frowning.

The CEO was shocked when he saw his expression each time he spoke about the numbers. I asked him whether he believed in the numbers he was sharing with his audience. He took a step back, lowered his head, and said, "No, I'm having a really hard time with these numbers; I'm not sure what the future holds for this business."

From the Heart

Then he asked if I could help him change the face he was making. My answer was an emphatic, "No!" But I told him I could help him craft a message around something he believed in, and when that happened, his body would follow. Once we aligned his message with his conviction, the body movements were authentic, the micro-expressions aligned, and the presentation was congruent.

When the CEO delivered his message to his team, he connected and even voiced his frustration to them. His courage to be authentic and transparent built trust with the team and fostered a richer conversation around the future of the business. The irony around his courage to be transparent is that the team already knew how the CEO felt. The trust wasn't built just because he shared his true feelings. Rather, his true feelings were given away through his micro-expressions, and the trust was built through the congruency of body and message.

The same is true with people around you. Those close to you, who know you well, know when you are forthright with them and when you're not. Sometimes it's best to call it out when someone is being inauthentic. Again, the key word here is *sometimes*. Remember, these tools are like the clubs in your golf bag. The techniques you choose will depend on where you are, who you are with, the levels of trust that exist or not, and so on.

It's easy to get excited about learning tips around influence because they can have an immediate impact. But I urge you to focus on the authentic message and believe in what you're talking about. In most cases that automatically creates congruent body language.

Record Everything

At age 18 I listened to my first sales-training cassette tape from the late Zig Ziglar. He said something extremely simple and profound: If you don't own a voice recorder, you haven't entered the world of professional selling.

So true. If you don't record your presentations often, you miss valuable learning and growth opportunities. It is one thing to try to remember what you said and how you said it. It is another thing to get feedback on what you said and how you said it. But it is another thing entirely to watch a video.

Every professional sporting team reviews film weekly not only of themselves but also of their competition. They analyze the film in detail, play by play, and then design plays based on consistencies and matchups. If you consider yourself a professional or aspire to be one in your profession, then I urge you to practice the same discipline.

Be Curious

Body language can be tricky. Various factors influence how we interpret specific body language, so be careful before making any judgments.

Clues, Not Absolutes

A good rule of thumb is that body language cues should lead to curiosity, not conclusions. When we are curious, we ask questions sincerely and with an open mind. For example, when we see a person with their arms crossed—often a sign of combativeness—we may ask them how they are feeling. They could respond that they're cold or perhaps feeling uncomfortable. This should make us more curious, so we adjust our approach to listen more rather than drive our message before our audience is ready to hear it.

When we make snap judgments based on too little information, we become annoying and intolerable. Accusing someone of being defensive because of one body language cue does not enhance one's influence. The goal isn't to read body language. The goal is connection, empathy, and trust.

Curiosity also works with self-reflection. We need to ask ourselves why we make a certain movement and what causes those micro-expressions. Then, like the CEO above, make the internal changes necessary to eliminate the *tells*.

Context Matters

As we've discussed, many contributing factors drive our behavior and affect how we sound to others. Stress affects body language and nonverbal cues. So does illness or emotional events such as divorce. When we're under pressure to perform or fear we're losing our job, that plays into how we communicate, too.

When assessing talent, each of us must decide how critical performance under pressure is to the job and whether it can be learned. I'll talk more about tools to master stress later.

Look for Clusters

Rather than making a judgment based on one nonverbal cue, look for clusters of information that either show congruency or incongruency with the language used. A simple example is the use of sarcasm.

"Oh yeah, I'm suuuuper excited to be here." Imagine a teenager who would prefer to be with friends saying that at a family dinner. The incongruency is that the words say one thing, but the tone says another. Most likely the words would be followed by an eye roll, possibly with arms crossed, and little facial expression. A cluster like that is pretty easy to decipher.

You're Being Watched

Daniel Goleman, PhD, author of *Emotional Intelligence: Why It Can Matter More than IQ*, made it clear that leaders are the most watched and listened to people in an organization. He describes a resonant leader as someone who understands that their emotional state, behavior, body language, and overall attitude are contagious and will infect an organization faster than a virus. Therefore, they must work diligently to grow their emotional intelligence so they can keep people focused on what matters most.[2]

When we focus on the body language and nonverbal cues of others, it's easy to forget how our behaviors affect them. We need to be diligent and attentive to the signals we send as well as receive. Are they congruent with the message we are trying to convey? One common example is the "My door is always open" mantra from leaders, who walk through the hallways with head down on the phone, not speaking to anyone.

If you're not paying attention to your body language and are unaware of any unintentional quirks or tics, you could be projecting a message that's the opposite of what you intend. And that can hinder sales, possible promotions, relationships, and even your physical safety.

The Hallway Walk

Someone once asked me what one thing I would choose to control or change within an organization that would have the biggest impact or influence on change. My answer was simple. Meetings. Meetings are where everyone is assembled, cultural norms are set, and relationships built or lost.

While working with the leadership team of a company with a billion-dollar commodity product, I asked where they make decisions that influence the organization. The team agreed that it was in their meetings. Then I asked how many people attend those meetings. The consensus was about 45 people.

"That's great," I said. "But what about the other 1,750 people in the company? Where do you interact with them?"

The team sat there with blank looks on their faces. Finally, someone muttered, "In the hallway?"

My follow-up question was, "What's your hallway walk?" How do you walk down the hallway? Do you make contact with people? Build relationships? Recognize people? Remember names? Or are you head down, rushing to your next meeting?"

The ensuing discussion led the company to begin a series of creative initiatives to help leaders and teams engage more throughout the day. That simple idea created more self-awareness among the leaders and the nonverbal signals that they may have been projecting unintentionally while simply walking down the hallway.

Critical Questions

Body language helps us decipher four critical questions:

- Are they embracing or rejecting me or the idea?
- Do they like or dislike me or the idea?
- Are they engaged or distracted?
- Are they being honest or lying?

These questions and their answers are key to the ability to influence and lead. They determine the outcome of interactions ranging from a first date to a second job interview. The answers to these questions can make or break a fundraising campaign pitch.

How we stand, how we use our hands, where our eyes focus, how our face moves, what we wear—all these nonverbal cues determine our fate. We need to be intentional and prepared.

First Impressions

What's more, those decisions usually are made in the **first three seconds.** At that point, most people have decided whether they **like** or **dislike** you. It's hard to influence someone who doesn't like you.

The brain is designed to make snap judgments based on first impressions. The brain decides whether it likes someone, whether it trusts someone, and whether it wants to work for or with a person, all based on how that person is perceived in an instant.

That may sound unfair, and it is. But it's reality, especially in today's digital world. Even more mind-boggling is we focus most of our energy on crafting the right words, yet research indicates that words alone barely begin to paint a picture of what's happening.[3]

In fact, the sound of our voices has a greater impact on first impressions.[4]

Our spoken words communicate information, but our body language and tone communicate our attitudes, feelings, and ultimately meaning. We must learn to look beyond the words.

Learned Skill

Unquestionably the most successful people are skilled at deciphering and managing the signals that our bodies send. Actors, for example, must learn to manage their body language to convince audiences that the role they are playing is real. When they do the job well, we suspend our disbelief and accept that the actor actually might be that character.

In business, we need to use appropriate body language to create the feelings, signals, and messages we want to send our colleagues. Without that alignment—words and body language conveying the same message—our audience won't trust us. They may not have the words or the conscious understanding to know why they don't trust us, but they will know something is off.

I enjoy asking others if they would like to read people's minds. Aside from the occasional holdout, almost everyone answers yes. To understand and read people's minds, we must learn to decipher and read their bodies because the body is an expression of the mind.

All the Details

Body language, after all, is the clearest window into our subconscious thoughts. We need to pay attention to its details to understand what people are truly feeling or how they are perceiving our messages.

When observing two people having a conversation, most people tend to watch the person speaking. Here's a challenge: The next time you see people talking, try not to watch the speaker but rather discreetly observe the listener. This indicates how the message is being received and offers information that most people miss. These little secrets can help you become more effective in connecting with people.

What's critical to understand, too, is that body language is a two-way street. As we constantly try to read people's body language—all the signals, such as posture, eye contact, and micro-expressions—we sometimes forget that we are sending messages to others who are consciously and subconsciously trying to read us.

It's not a matter of whether we are sending signals, but whether we are sending the right ones. If we don't pay attention and are unaware of unintended body language quirks or tics, we could project a message at odds with what we intend. That can affect our sales calls, interviews, first dates, and even virtual meetings.

The Eyes

We've all heard that the eyes are the windows to the soul. In communication, they are the windows to meaning and one of the best ways to indicate interest or disinterest. In fact, we send more messages with our eyes than any other part of our body, which is why professional poker players wear sunglasses in tournaments. We also know that a genuine smile happens in conjunction with the eyes.

Our eyes are one of the most powerful tools in our tool bag. They create trust and safety and can be used to build bridges with people. When we truly care about the person we are speaking with, our eyes will reveal our feelings. When we are passionate about the topic of a presentation, our eyes will sparkle, and our audience will see that. These physiological responses are virtually impossible to fake and as we mentioned before, occur when we are being genuine.

First Impressions

Suppose you're on a sales call with someone you've never met, and you show up in mirrored shades, and hand them a proposal. That's not the best first impression. In that scenario you project a frame that says you're hiding behind the shades and unwilling to connect.

The eyes are a crucial part of human connection. Micro-movements in the eyes communicate meaning, and people want to see that meaning to connect for trust. People who wear glasses especially need to be aware of this. Removing one's glasses for the first few minutes or even first few seconds of a meeting can help someone connect more quickly with their audience. It only takes about 7 to 15 seconds to achieve a good first impression. (More on that later.)

The Glare Effect

In certain situations, especially video presentations and calls, glasses create reflections and distortions that easily blur or hide the eye connection. Worse, some glasses can create a jarring reflection that bothers viewers. (Note to self: Bald heads also can cause rough reflections that bother an audience, especially on video.)

Test your glasses in front of a screen to see whether they project a glare. Wherever you do video calls, try making a video recording of yourself—even using a cell phone on FaceTime or other function—to study the image you project. Move your face around to various positions to see how your glasses look on the screen. Some shapes and sizes of glasses are less reflective than others. Some people also have a special pair of less reflective glasses designated for presentations and/or video use.

Even those people who need their glasses to see well should ditch them initially. Then claim the frame: After first impressions have been established, say something like, "It's great to meet you," overcompensate with a big smile and say, "I hope it's not too much of a reflection, but I need to wear my glasses so I can see you. Is that OK?"

Digital Body Language

The pandemic not only changed the way we work but also the world of body language. In today's virtual and hybrid world we must consider our digital body language and how we communicate through a small screen. There's not much room even with two screens—one to see our audience and the other our presentation.

In many cases, we're unintentionally sending the message of disinterest because we're looking at someone's face instead of directly into the camera. Adding to that, most of us deal with bad lighting, poor audio, and often a mediocre camera.

Light and Shadows

Beyond the glasses and glare, video chats are notorious for presenting participants in unflattering light, literally. To connect to an audience, they have to see you clearly.

Unfortunately, as simple as it sounds, proper lighting often is overlooked. How do you feel when you're introduced to someone in shady light? Chances are you tend to think the person might be a little shady, too. No matter how many lights it takes to create optimal lighting in your video chat space, get them. Another illuminating tip: Face a window rather than have it behind you.

Positioning

For those who think this detail is a waste, again be a student of your own experience. Experiment with different lighting and camera angles by walking around with a cell phone camera turned toward you. You'll be amazed at how different you appear depending on the lighting and camera angles.

Again, pay attention to how your image appears on a screen. Think about how you feel on a video or video call when someone only shows a small part of their head, perhaps at the bottom of the screen. Then compare that with how you feel when a camera/screen is positioned in such a way that the person fills the screen and has a solid presence. If you were taking a selfie in an empty room, you likely wouldn't position a small picture of your face in the corner with the rest of the frame dominated up by the ceiling. It's the same with video presentations, chats, meetings, and one-on-one video conversations.

Make sure your microphone is placed optimally, too. Too far away or the wrong angle, and your audience will disassociate with you and your message.

Think about the image you convey to others from the first seconds to the last. If you can see the floor, the camera angle is too high.

These concerns don't reflect personal vanity. Each is about eye connection and the potential for disassociation. If your audience is distracted, if they can't hear or see you clearly, they won't listen. And, if they're not listening, they can't get your message.

Words Aren't Enough

The meaning behind emotions is understood more easily when we consider the 7-38-55 rule. It was formulated by Albert Mehrabian, PhD, now a professor emeritus of psychology at the University of California, Los Angeles, in his 1971 book *Silent Messages*.

Mehrabian's rule states that 7 percent of meaning is communicated through spoken word, 38 percent through tone of voice, and 55 percent through nonverbals.[5]

I grew up around this study. (In Figure 10.1, see the photo of my mother using Mehrabian's rule in her work to help community organizations in South Florida.)

The Power of Inflection

Mehrabian's numbers help us understand that the true meaning of communication can change when tone and body language changes. For example, if I said, "I didn't say he ate the cake" with no unique inflection (emphasis on a particular word), you would likely understand me clearly.

Figure 10.1

However, if I changed my tone and inflection and emphasized different words, the true meaning of the sentence changes. Mehrabian says 38 percent of meaning is communicating that way. Try saying aloud the sentences below with emphasis on the highlighted word and listening to the difference in the meaning conveyed.

1. "**I** didn't say he ate the cake."
2. "I didn't **say** he ate the cake."
3. "I didn't say **he** ate the cake."
4. "I didn't say he **ate** the cake."
5. "I didn't say he ate the **cake**."

Especially relevant to the body language discussion is that Mehrabian found that nonverbals made up 55 percent of the meaning in communication. Again, as discussed, that's more support for the fact that when someone's words say one thing and their body another, we are more likely to listen to or believe their body.

Even more fascinating is that when we combine tone and nonverbals, according to Mehrabian's numbers, they make up 93 percent of the impact on emotional meaning.

Words Still Matter

A big word of caution, however: Mehrabian's study often is misquoted and misinterpreted. What his study means is that if someone has great words but their nonverbals or tone send the wrong message, no one will bother to hear what they have to offer.

So if someone's meetings are boring or if they speak in a boring monotone, don't expect an audience to hear their message, no matter how valuable it is.

We must learn to be dynamic, to move our bodies in the right manner, to understand facial expressions, and to manage our tone of voice. We don't want to minimize the importance of words in relation to body language. All cues have a function in the equation of communication. The most trusted indicator of true meaning, however, is nonverbal communication.

Self-Awareness and the Little Things

Self-awareness also plays a big role in nonverbal communication. Seeing how those nonverbals happen isn't always easy because unless we record ourselves or watch ourselves in the mirror, much of our behavior is subconscious.

Takes Practice

The good news is that with practice and discipline, and through recording and reviewing our presentations, we can develop a keen awareness of our body language. Trusted and respected individuals offering frequent feedback also helps.

We can learn to control our body language and be more intentional in our movements as well as sharpen our senses to read and respond to others' body language. These are the building blocks of emotional intelligence.

The way we respond affects our personal brand, our relationships, and our ability to influence. Without the skills and awareness, we risk jeopardizing important aspects of our success in life by handing them over to our subconscious behaviors.

The Little Things

Mastery of these skills begins by learning to pay attention to movements, gestures, and all the things that normally seem unimportant such as changing behaviors and slight voice changes, facial expressions, and even the direction someone's feet point. These are giveaways to the message that's trying to be sent and more importantly, the meaning behind the message.

Of course we can't control every nuance, so we need to narrow our focus to what's practical to control, those movements we make regularly in everyday life. We build an awareness of how we move, how we stand, facial expressions, tone of voice, and how we respond to others.

Can't Fake It

The good—and bad depending on perspective—news is that body language can't be easily faked. Consider all the voluntary and involuntary muscles in our bodies or even just our faces. All that's impossible to control all the time.

No matter how good someone thinks they are at controlling body language, how aware and in tune they are to their bodies, there will be *leakage*. That's the involuntary signals and movements, the subconscious giveaways or tells as they are known in poker. Those are the nuances that reveal someone's true feelings. Think in terms of the CEO earlier in the chapter whose microexpression revealed his true feelings about the numbers.

But the coolest part—some people might say the scariest part—is that this all happens outside of the realm of consciousness. These are subconscious actions, and our bodies don't ask permission to send a tell.

Therefore, the more we know about body language, the more clearly we see and understand that it is the most reliable indicator of a person's true meaning, feelings, attitudes, and emotions.

Practice Like a Pro

Research examining the meaning behind our movements and facial expressions is limited. Instead, we're left to learn it on our own.

As mentioned previously, the best way to master body movements is through recording yourself. Or if the goal is to improve your voice, record it on video as well because your posture and facial expressions affect how you sound. Anyone with a smart phone can do that these days. Just prop the phone up in front of you or place it on a tripod and start recording. Try a mock sales presentation, too.

Pay attention to your appearance, how you stand, how you talk, the angle of your head, your hands. Do you have any nervous movements that distract from your message or, worse, send the wrong message? Do you fidget? How might you improve all of the above? Is your weight balanced? Do you sway?

Would you buy from you? If not, why not? Would you listen to you? Would you trust you? All of this contributes to the message you deliver to your audience.

With video you can watch not only how you move initially but also how you respond to various cues and other things you might never catch through your own self-awareness.

Whether with video or audio, critically review and study yourself. Then try it again and again, practicing how to improve.

Presence

We know that our thoughts affect our bodies. When we are sad, we slouch, head down, turned inward on ourselves. But what about the other way around? Can our bodies affect our mind—can our physiology affect how we feel?

The research says, yes, it can. For example, upright posture is a sign of and projects positive energy; slouching, just the opposite.[6]

Posture First

One of the main reasons to focus on posture is that we have direct control over it. When someone is asked to raise their right hand, assuming they don't have an injury or handicap preventing it, they do so immediately. But we don't have direct control over our nervous system, so we take the indirect approach through the body.

Let's think in terms of logos (logic). If we change our body, we change the emotions. When we change our emotions, we can change the decisions we make. When we make new decisions to better our lives, we improve the quality of life.

The same applies to an audience. That's why I ask my audiences to stand before I start my keynote speeches. The action changes the audience's internal chemistry and wakes them up. Getting an audience physically involved is a good thing. It invests that audience in the process, moves the energy, gets the blood flowing, and creates positive feelings associated with the presenter's message.

Baby Steps

Presence is a choice that requires consistency over time. The small changes accumulate over time to direct how we feel. I was born pigeon-toed and had to wear corrective shoes as a kid. Over the years I learned to force my feet to open, consciously stand with my chest out, and keep my chin higher.

Over time, those little steps accumulated. Nonetheless, as an adult, I have to be mindful of how I stand.

Don't Be an Empty Suit

Social media makes it easy to pick and choose what we show the world. Instagram is basically a highlight reel. But in person, people see through the charade and can smell a manufactured impression.

Real presence comes from an unshakable belief in ourselves. That confidence appears effortless and natural because it is. It's not easy to achieve, and sometimes we must force our bodies into positions of power and presence before we emotionally feel powerful. But that discipline is essential to develop presence over time.

As I mentioned earlier, the best basketball coach I ever had, Ricky Suggs, used to say to me, "A good shooter is either on or he's going to be on. Keep shooting!" I believe that philosophy applies here too. A powerful leader's presence is either "on" or it's going to be "on," so keep standing strong.

Nervousness Is OK

We focus so much attention on trying to overcome nervousness for fear of appearing weak or lacking confidence. But the reality is that confidence and stress are not mutually exclusive. They can coexist and quite often do.

For example, the body may communicate that it's nervous, while the person pretends they are fine. That's when the audience loses trust. The irony is that the person who acknowledges their nervousness and proceeds anyway is seen not only as brave but also as confident and more trustworthy. Nervousness also can be endearing and creates a powerful connection to the audience.

Studies show that powerful people have common behavior patterns, which include:

- Greater eye contact;
- Speaking more slowly;
- Pausing more often;
- Taking up more space physically;
- Sitting and walking upright and not hunched over.

These traits should become a to-do list for people who want to improve and develop their presence. Following are some helpful steps on the journey to greater presence:

- Practice making more eye contact in every conversation. Hold that eye contact for as long as possible without making the situation awkward or intimidating.
- Pay attention to the pace of a speech or presentation. Slow it down so that you have greater control of your voice.
- Be mindful of utilizing powerful pauses instead of run-on sentences and filler words.
- Intentionally try to take up more space when sitting or standing. Don't be rude or obnoxious, just be bigger and wider. Move around more and don't be afraid to be more animated with your arms when telling a story.
- Walk as tall as possible with your chest out. Practice and record it so you don't look ridiculous. With practice and the right mindset, the posture will become natural and powerful.

These subtle changes in your posture and walking with more pride and strength will trigger more hormones that lead to confidence and presence.

Back to the Basics

- *Smile big and with your eyes;*
- *Make appropriate eye contact;*
- *Manage comfortable distance;*
- *Sit and stand straight;*
- *Keep your shoulders back and chest open;*
- *Raise your chin slightly but not too high;*
- *Keep a balanced stance with your feet shoulder-width apart;*
- *Never stand behind the podium while speaking;*
- *Have purposeful movement that contributes to your message;*
- *Speak powerfully, projecting your voice;*
- *Use pauses to allow an audience to paint the picture.*

The Hand Conundrum

What should I do with my hands? We've all been there whether at in-person meetings and presentations or on video. People just don't know what to do with their hands, where to position them when talking to others. And, yes, there are right and wrong positions that convey the right or the wrong message.

The Influence Zone

When attending an in-person meeting, everyone has what's known as the influence zone (see Figure 10.2). That zone is in

IN-PERSON INFLUENCE ZONE

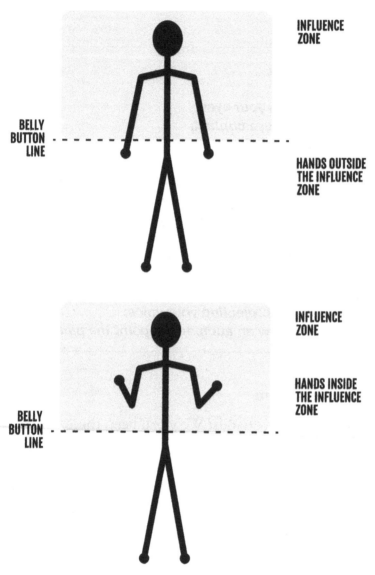

Figure 10.2

front of you and extends upward from your belly button to your eyes. When your hands are in the influence zone, you're more engaging. Your message transmits. Move the hands out of the influence zone, to your sides, perhaps, and you lose influence.

An optimal place for your hands is home base—hands together with fingers loosely intertwined, centered just above or at the belly button level, and with your shoulders square. That's "home base" because a person leaves home base to use their hands and make gestures, and then comes back home. This gives you a place to put your hands while keeping your shoulders square inside the influence zone.

If a speaker doesn't use their hands or uses awkward hand movements, an audience will label them as distant and cold, according to a study that appeared in the *Leadership and Organization Development Journal*.[7]

A few don'ts when it comes to your hands:

- Using an upward pointing steeple, which comes across as conniving;
- Pointing with fingers, which conveys aggressiveness;
- Drumming your fingers, which is highly distracting;
- Making a fist or fists, which communicates stress;
- Crossing your arms in front of you, which signals that you are closed off;
- Keeping arms at your sides loosely, which looks sloppy;
- Using any self-soothing or hand massaging, which conveys nervousness;
- Picking in ears, eyes, or nose, which is obviously gross.

All these hand positions convey the wrong message and certainly aren't conducive to messaging or closing a deal.

Virtual Influence Zone for Videos

Understand, too, that on video or a video call where the hands aren't visible at home base, the influence zone can change slightly. Depending on the size of the picture, you may need to move your hands higher.

Sometimes you feel a little like a T-rex, and that's OK. Study your image on the screen and move your hands higher or lower as necessary keeping in mind that you want to convey an image of communication and trust.

Just Relax

The bottom line is we need to understand the image and the emotion we convey to our audience. We need to first relax and be conscious of how we project ourselves.

The goal is to command the stage with your presence and posture and step into the audience with your body language.

Study yourself in the mirror. Better still, make a video recording of yourself or take a selfie. What do you see? Your audience sees that, too, and reacts accordingly. If you look tense, your audience feels the tension. If you look relaxed, your audience sees that, too.

You Are the PowerPoint Slide

The PowerPoint I'm referring to isn't Microsoft's slideshow app on a computer or handheld. It's you, the communicator and influencer. You are the PowerPoint; all eyes are on you.

And Not

Unlike Microsoft's PowerPoint with its neat little animations that everyone likes, the animations we display in front of others aren't as popular. In fact, they're distractions.

These are the nervous tics and shifts that distract the audience in a presentation or one-on-one discussion. Maybe it's an unconscious weight shift from side to side. Or perhaps a flick of the hair, toss of the head, lost eye contact, or staring at the ground. Playing with a pen, pencil, or other object is a common subconscious action, too.

Whatever someone's personal animations, all are irritants that can prompt an audience to disassociate and lose interest. And if they're not interested, they're not listening, and if they're not listening, the speaker isn't influencing.

When you make a new point, you change the presentation slide. If you are the presentation visual, then move your body to a different position on the stage or in the room when you make a new point.

Too often speakers have cement in their shoes and never move. Use the stage with purpose, and time your movements to make it feel smooth.

Banish the Irritants

The good news is you can learn to control these annoying animations. Again, it's about being self-aware. First, pay attention to your animations. Think consciously about them, and figure out how to control them.

When you learn to calm down and feel comfortable in front of audiences, often you can better control those animations, too.

Powerful Takeaways

- People make snap judgments based on first impressions. That's why body language is central to the influence tool set.
- Nonverbal clues such as tone of voice, eye contact, inflection, and how close we stand to someone are cues that convey specific messages and affect our influence.

- Look for clusters of nonverbal cues before making a judgment.
- The eyes are windows into what we communicate.
- In today's virtual and hybrid world we must consider our digital body language and how we communicate through a small screen.
- Self-awareness plays a big role in nonverbal communication.
- We must learn to pay attention to movements, gestures, and all the things that normally seem unimportant such as changing behaviors and slight voice changes, facial expressions, and even the direction someone's feet point. These are giveaways to the message that's trying to be sent, and more importantly, the meaning behind the message.
- With video you can watch not only how you move initially but also how you respond to various cues and other things you might never catch through your own self-awareness.
- Real presence comes from an unshakable belief in ourselves. That confidence appears effortless and natural because it is.
- Confidence and stress can coexist and quite often do.
- An optimal place for your hands is home base—hands together with fingers loosely intertwined, centered just above or at the belly button level, and with your shoulders square.
- We need to understand the image and the emotion we convey to our audience. We need to first relax and be conscious of how we project ourselves.
- The goal is to command the stage with your presence and posture and step into the audience with your body language.

11

Interpersonal Communication: LOVE and Other Things

"The single biggest problem in communication is the illusion that it has taken place."

—*George Bernard Shaw,*
Irish playwright and author[1]

NOT EVERYONE WANTS to stand up in front of hundreds or thousands of people and influence them with a message. But all of us want to influence someone one-on-one. Whether it's a parent trying to connect with a child, a teacher to a student, manager to employee, potential suitor to a person of interest, CEO to their company's teams, or a sales professional to a prospect, mastering the art of conversation has a massive impact on relationships and the ability to influence.

Unfortunately, the skill of how to be a good conversationalist has become a lost art form for many. The professionals we work with often want to know more and better ways to connect and converse with others. That's why I've developed a natural sequence on how to connect with others comfortably. When we master this art, we can take a cold relationship and warm it relatively quickly.

189

A powerful sequence that follows what the best communicators do is all about LOVE. That's an acronym for:

- Listen;
- Observe;
- Validate;
- Expand.

Before we get into LOVE, let's look more closely at communication itself.

The Communication Challenge

Communication is part of every human interaction. That's why people want to become better communicators. But communication is tough. And as we've mentioned, it's even tougher under stress. Yet many of us think we're great conversationalists no matter the circumstances.

It's Personal

How well do you communicate? Most people respond to that question with a positive assessment of their skills while simultaneously being open to more learning.

Look at your skill level another way. What would a significant other, coworker, child, friend, boss, or customer say about the effectiveness of your communication? Instead of a quick answer, consider whether that person will even tell the truth. If you think so, read on.

First, we must become aware that no matter how good a communicator we think we are, the reality is we are ineffective at communication. To truly understand that, we must recognize what often goes unnoticed.

The concept of *communication* has been so widely discussed, misunderstood, and overused that it has almost become a cliché. The 20th-century film director Stanley Kubrick shared an underlying challenge when dealing with clichés: "If you can talk brilliantly about a problem, it can create the consoling illusion that it has been mastered."[2]

In other words, when it comes to communication, most of us can talk a great game, but in terms of follow-through, the research and experience show that we stumble most of the time.

Understanding the Problem

Before we dive into what needs to change, let's examine the problem. The dictionary defines communication as the act or process of using words, sounds, signs, or behaviors to express or exchange information or to express your ideas, thoughts, or feelings to someone else.[3]

By definition we communicate all the time. Public relations theorists James E. Grunig and Larissa A. Grunig define *excellent communication* as communication that is managed strategically, meets its objectives, and balances the needs of the organization and the needs of key people with two-way symmetrical communication.[4]

That definition, though, doesn't help understand the difficulty of being perceived as an effective communicator.

The Illusion

When we combine the wisdom of Kubrick and Shaw, it becomes clear that the biggest threat to good communication lies in our perceptions that trick us into thinking we have communicated effectively or that we have understood clearly. The worst of this is that our perceptions form our reality. In other words, if we aren't diligent in maintaining a high sense of awareness, we will never know when we communicate poorly.

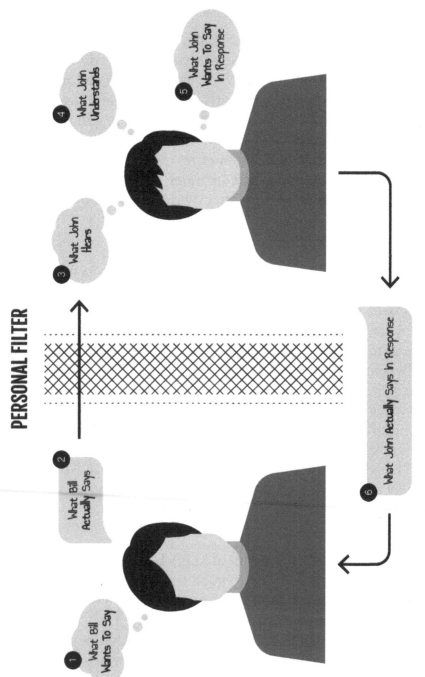

Study this simple conversation between Bill and John. If at any point the steps in the process break down, there is potential for a wide range of miscommunication.

The challenge then becomes how to fix something that most of us aren't aware exists. It starts with the fact that much of what we take for granted, including how we communicate, is often very complex when analyzed. For example, anytime we communicate something, there are six checkpoints in our brain that a message must pass through before it is fully transmitted. At any of these points, our message can either pass in its intended form or become distorted. The checkpoints include:

1. What I **want** to say;
2. What I **actually** say;
3. What the other person **hears;**
4. What the other person **understands;**
5. What the other person **wants to say in response;**
6. What the other person **actually says in response.**

This is just one exchange of one thought. A typical conversation has dozens, if not hundreds of back-and-forth exchanges, each with the potential that the message can be lost.

One lost message leads to further misunderstanding, which can further distort the message. We've all watched or participated in the telephone game where a message starts off one way and ends up sounding nothing like its original form.

Filters and More

Instagram took the world by storm when it introduced filters that made us all instant professional photographers. Then filters gave us the ability to transform how our faces looked. We could basically choose any look. Find a blemish? No problem, there's a filter to eliminate that. Want darker skin complexion? There's a filter for that. Want a stronger jaw line? There's a filter for that, too.

We now can distort how people perceive us aesthetically as long as they don't see us in person.

On a Personal Note

Interpersonal communication has filters that accomplish the same thing but also include what we say and how we are perceived holistically. Your personal filter is the way you see, engage with, and understand the world around you and inside you.

Those filters are the result of the frame you construct and how you interpret the world. Similar to how Instagram filters change the original photo, personal filters can completely distort the intended message. What makes this so challenging is that myriad factors play into the equation.

Filters impact everything we hear, read, and consume in life. Pessimists see events through a negative lens, creating a negative reality. People who see the world through an optimistic lens likely find the silver lining even in the most difficult times.

Filters also affect how we explain life and events. The narratives we tell ourselves play a major role in our happiness and ability to cope with day-to-day setbacks. If we believe we are healthy, we make healthy decisions and have a healthy behavior because they are part of our healthy story. This personal narrative of being healthy affects the way we engage with the world, and that influences the way we view the world. It's a self-perpetuating cycle that starts with our very first thought.

Filters in Communication

Let's assume that Lynn is an excellent communicator and can translate what she *wants* to say into what she *actually* says. That information still must pass through her listener's personal filters. Those filters form an invisible barrier that can distort even a seemingly clear message from Lynn.

Common filters include the emotional state, cultural background, situational context, personal beliefs, and stress level of the listener. These filters will influence the perception and interpretation of Lynn's message, resulting in either a clear communication or a distorted one.

Let's examine the personal filters more closely.

Emotional state.   We are always in an emotional state. How that affects our ability to interpret what we hear and react to the message depends on the emotional state of the moment—joyful, anxious, upset, expectant, excited, sad, and so on.

When we are upset or anxious, it is much harder to receive new ideas. Conversely, when we are joyful or expectant and looking forward to hearing what someone has to say, we listen better and are more likely to accept reasonable ideas if they are presented well.

Cultural background.   Personal history; country, state, or city of origin; and upbringing have an enormous impact on our filters. Different accents or word choices can confuse understanding of difficult concepts as well as interpretation of events, tone, facial expressions, and the like. When formulating important messages, we should consider cultures, customs, and histories that are different from our own.

Situational context.   Recent experiences and environmental factors also influence the way we receive messages. Unlike emotions, situational context involves elements external to the listener. That includes how a message is presented and what was said or done previously. For example, a room that is too noisy, dark, cold, or uncomfortable will distract the listener's attention. Remember earlier when I was presenting at a noisy luncheon meeting and claimed the frame by getting a distracted audience to listen?

Personal beliefs. In life, everything we experience is related to previous experiences. When we understand an idea or concept, it is because we are relating it to our past learning. Truly new experiences are a rarity.

We have core beliefs that guide the way we listen, perceive, and interpret what we hear. That's why it's important to be aware of our listeners' personal beliefs. We need to select our words carefully and craft presentations and communications that can touch our listeners on a deeper emotional level, which is where the most effective communication is achieved.

Stress level. Under stress, our brain becomes highly selective about what it allows us to perceive. This phenomenon, while vital to protect us from physical danger, can make it difficult to listen and accurately interpret what is being said.

An example of how our personal filters affect a message are fans at a sporting event. We've all seen a referee make a certain call and watched how fans react. The fan whose team benefited argues that it was fair and the right call, while the fan whose team was penalized derides the call as horrible and wrong.

Two groups of people receiving the same message yet having opposite interpretations and subsequent reactions. The same happens in politics. An event is filtered through different political parties and ends up delivering a different message to each party.

Countermeasures?

Filters are strong. We need to recognize that and understand that different listeners don't always hear the speaker's intended message. Although it's impossible to remove these filters completely, we can mitigate their influence.

Consider this analogy from the world of mathematics. How do we know that 2 times 3 equals 6? We can check our answer by dividing 6 by 3, which equals 2.

So how can we check our *communication* to make sure our message got through? To ensure that our message is received as intended our audience/listener needs to repeat the message back in some manner.

Being Right versus Being Heard

Miscommunication is often caused by misinterpreting the intended needs of people.

We assume that people need to feel like they are always right. But after years of facilitating thousands of conversations, I have learned that's an inaccurate assumption. Instead, people really want to feel that they have been heard. That can only be determined by them, not us.

For that to happen, we must provide the space for someone to confirm or deny that they've been heard, and if not, give them the opportunity to try again. That sounds easy enough and is *if* no stress is involved. After all, when we aren't stressed, conversations are easy. The real value of this knowledge is apparent when we are stressed.

Imagine that you're upset and someone complains that you aren't hearing or listening to them. Do you have the emotional maturity, discipline, intelligence, or even grace at that point to let go of all you're feeling to make sure they feel heard? In reality, most people don't. But if the goal is for people to hear you and if you can see beyond this moment of resistance, a topic we will cover in chapter 12, then maybe the best move is to put aside your personal feelings momentarily. Whether you do or don't, it's important to understand what's happening. If your goal is influence, there's only one choice: make your audience feel heard first.

Tips for Effective Communication

- **Ask clarifying questions:** In addition to indicating interest and attention, these questions can clarify meaning and may unearth multiple messages. Some approaches that foster clarification are:
  - o I'm not sure I understand.
  - o What was it you just said?
  - o What do you mean by . . .
- **Paraphrase:** Do not assume you understand what was said. Paraphrase to test whether you heard right and to show your depth of understanding. For example:
  - o Do you mean that . . .
- **Repeat back what you heard:** In a stressful situation, don't over-paraphrase. Try to be verbatim, and always ask, "Am I correct?" or "Is that right?" Give the other person the opportunity to respond. We have done this exercise with more than 100,000 people, and almost all were shocked at how often the answer was no. One of the most common reactions was, "I never knew how hard it was to really listen."
- **Check perception:** Remember that people also communicate feelings through language. A perception check should not express approval or disapproval of someone's feelings but rather should convey an understanding of the feelings. For example, Jim says, "I get the impression that you are bored. Am I correct?" And Bill responds, "No, it's very hot in here, and I'm uncomfortable. That's why I keep moving around."
- **Active, attentive listening:** This kind of listening takes practice and is an essential communication skill. Perfect practice of active listening involves being responsive through

facial expression, eye contact, and obvious interest. To demonstrate your keen interest, use the following phrases:

o I see;
o Yes;
o Please go on.

One-on-One Communication

We have all met someone who is an enjoyable conversationalist. Time flies, we laugh, we go deep, we bond, we discuss meaningful topics, and we grow from the encounter. Trust is built, and we are eager to talk again. Is it magic? Is it random chemistry? Or is it a formula?

After studying communication for many years and practicing with thousands of people, I believe there is a formula and a sequence to it all. Remember, the right sequence to connect is all about LOVE, an acronym for:

- Listen;
- Observe;
- Validate;
- Expand.

Communication is a broad topic, so let's just focus on one part—one-on-one conversation. Some people refer to this as the art of being a conversationalist.

I learned how important the skill is after spending years traveling the country training sales professionals on how to make cold calls. I enjoy cold calling because when we understand why it's cold, we can warm it up easily with some minor adjustments in approach, language, and most important, personal philosophy.

Fear of Rejection

The main reason people don't achieve more of what they want in life is the fear of rejection. That's especially true in sales and dating. It happens as well when you're calling that big prospect who could change your career or striking up a simple conversation with that person who caught your eye in the grocery.

Both situations create the same internal chemical whirlwind that leaves us at a loss for words and sounding like a bumbling idiot. For most people, the feared result is completely debilitating and prevents them from making the approach.

You Create the Fear

Let's analyze why rejection is even part of the communication equation.

Why do we feel perfectly comfortable speaking with friends at happy hour but crumble if asked to say the same thing in front of a room of people? Why can we approach a stranger in a store for directions with no problem, but if we especially like someone and want to spark up a conversation, our entire demeanor changes? The answers to those questions are based on the fact that in one scenario we have a hidden agenda and in the other we don't.

The Hidden Agenda

People ask me all the time if the AMPLIFII principles work in dating. And the answer is, "Absolutely." That comment usually follows a conversation that basically asserts, "Nice guys finish last." The reality is that "nice guys" don't finish last. "Nice guys" are passive manipulative liars.

That's a hard fact for many people to digest. The reason they are passive manipulative liars is that they hope that being nice will get them something in exchange. If they challenge me, I simply ask them why they specifically choose to be nice to one person but not another. That's when they drop their shoulders and realize that maybe this passive unintentionally manipulative approach won't get them very far.

Humans have an aversion to anyone who tries to hide their true intention with fake behavior. The same is true when a salesperson makes a cold call. The prospect can smell the phoniness a mile away. The same thing happens when a child needs something from a parent and acts overly sweet. We are programmed to spot this behavior immediately.

Leaders fall into this trap all the time when speaking to their teams. The façade in front of a group that doesn't match the one-on-one experience is a sure way to destroy trust and credibility (ethos).

Stop Trying to Be Liked

The reason we aren't stressed or rejected at happy hour with our friends is because we aren't trying to make them like us. The reason we ask a stranger for directions is we don't have the hidden agenda of asking for a date. When we remove that hidden element, the fear of rejection magically goes away.

We can sum up most of the examples above and most failed conversations with the hidden agenda of one person trying to get another to like them. When a person enters the conversation with the goal of being liked—consciously or subconsciously—the conversation inherently takes a different form. Name-dropping, humble bragging, resumes, and other ways of saying, "I hope you like me" dominate the conversation leaving little room for connection and every opportunity for rejection.

Start Liking People

To authentically connect with others this process requires us to let go of the need to be liked and start *proactively* liking other people. If we enter a conversation with the intent of finding a reason to like someone, the dynamics change. Our tone, line of questioning, pacing, and ability to listen all are different, and the other person feels it.

Because we aren't trying to get something or asking for anything, there is nothing to reject. If there is nothing to reject, then there is nothing to fear.

Plenty of studies look at why we tend to feel more comfortable around people who like us. The reasons range from consensual validation, shared commonalities, and certainty of being liked to more fun, enjoyable interactions, and the ability to be more like ourselves. All these reasons lead back to one thing we learned early on in this book—the feeling of safety.

The LOVE Method

By now it's clear that our ability to connect with others is a big part of influence. Therefore, often when we work with professionals they want to know more and better ways to connect and converse with others.

What Is It?

I came up with the LOVE method after years of people asking how is it that I can connect with people so quickly. I realized that four things in sequence and on repeat make the difference. And I realized that the best leaders, managers, parents, sales professionals, and conversationalists do the same thing.

This applies to any conversation. When we master this process, we can take a cold relationship and warm it relatively quickly. We can take current relationships that may be in a rut and revitalize them. The applications are endless.

The LOVE method, as mentioned, earlier is:

- Listen;
- Observe;
- Validate;
- Expand.

This sounds relatively straightforward and easy. But following through on the sequential process and doing it right is tough and, as usual, takes practice. It also involves unlearning what we already know and do.

Listen

One of the biggest mistakes businesspeople make as communicators is forgetting to listen and actually hear what their customers say. When we really listen, we can formulate a better response. As I mentioned earlier, we can't plant seeds in cement. We need to lay the groundwork first.

We could do an entire book on the art of listening. Think about all the emotions involved, the body language, and the distractions that pull us away from being able to listen empathetically.

Clear mind.   One of the secrets to listening is the ability to clear our minds and listen without an agenda. That means instead of the typical crafting of a response while someone talks, we should listen to what is being said. After all, that's what we all strive for in the study of influence. We want people to listen to our messages. We can't expect others to listen unless we're willing to listen first.

What makes this approach difficult to master is that initially it triggers the internal fear, "Will I be ready to respond" or "Will

I know the next question to ask?" In a social setting it's easy and natural to keep the conversation going. But in business—a sales presentation, speech, or board meeting, for example—it's as if we're tongue-tied and suddenly can't think.

Center of attention.   Listening with the LOVE approach also requires us to maintain focus on the individual with whom we are speaking. The normal tendency is to craft a response that removes the focus from the speaker.

Consider the following two scenarios:

Scenario 1:

> Speaker: Where are you from?
>
> Audience of one: Hawaii.
>
> Speaker: Oh, I love that place. My favorite beach is . . .

Scenario 2:

> Speaker: Where are you from?
>
> Audience of one: Hawaii.
>
> Speaker: Oh, that's so cool. What is your favorite part about Hawaii?

In Scenario 1, the speaker quickly has shifted the spotlight away from the audience of one. Suddenly, the conversation focuses back on the speaker, losing the potential connection with the audience. People think this is relating to the other person when actually it's one-upping someone. This is where good intention goes awry.

In Scenario 2, though, the speaker continues the focus on the audience of one. The key—and the challenge—is to not draw the spotlight from the other person. Even if we have been to Hawaii 20 times and have 100 stories to tell that could relate, we should wait and keep asking questions with the goal of learning more.

This allows the other person to share more and lets us learn more about what there is to like about them. As the conversation progresses, we will have our chance to share experiences. But we must make the connection first and keep the spotlight on the other person as long as possible.

Observe

When we listen the right way, we also observe. That includes physically observing body language and how it matches the tone of voice as well as the other nonverbal messages someone sends when they speak.

If we don't observe, we may miss that key clue to the real message. It could be a missed eyeroll or inflection that totally changes the message's meaning. The right kind of listening also means leaning into the person who is talking. It's a physical act that conveys we are paying attention.

People often miss these subtle cues. In a sales presentation or a speech, the audience sends out those signals constantly. If we're not observing, we disconnect and become an out-of-touch leader. Remember, no one follows a leader who is out of touch.

We should look for points of passion as well as similar likes. The place where our passions intersect will be a fun place to continue dialogue and build relationships.

Validate

As mentioned earlier, we all need to feel we have value. We want people to listen to our messages. That's why following the sequence of the brain using the AMPLIFII formula and the LOVE method matters. Validation is one of the most important and often missed elements in creating that feeling of trust and being valued in conversation.

Validation is authentically reflecting back in some way what that person said that influenced us. Lean in, brighten that smile, nod the head, and show enthusiasm and excitement with words and actions. Some responses could include:

- "Oh, cool."
- "Awesome."
- "I didn't know that!"
- "That's disgusting!" (With a laugh.)

The latter is a great way to offer validation when someone is talking about a food they genuinely dislike. It shows honesty and trustworthiness.

This honesty and trust are even more crucial in today's virtual world. We constantly must validate that we listen and hear what's being said.

If we omit the validation, our conversations sound like an interrogation. We also must realize that our conversations—at least in the beginning—aren't necessarily a two-way street.

Expand

Too often conversations skip along the waterline and never go deeper. They're superficial and fail to connect with the other person. Instead, we need to go beneath surface-level topics that do nothing to reveal who we are and what we value. We do that by learning to expand our interactions through asking the right questions, paying attention to the details, and engaging the other person.

The main reason people don't do well at presentations, in cold calls, or in conversations as discussed earlier, is because they try to get people to like them instead of digging to find reasons to proactively like others. We do that by bombarding them with information in the hopes that some of it may get them to like us more. The result is a boring, one-sided conversation that never amounts to anything. When that happens in any persuasive or influence scenario, people notice it, raise their natural resistance, and make connection even more difficult.

Being proactive about finding things we like is the key component. That happens when we tap into our curiosity about people. Some things to consider:

- What makes someone tick?
- What do they value?
- Why does someone do what they do?
- What are their passions?

When we find those cues and ask expanding questions, a conversation digs deeper to find the thread that uncovers the passion.

People say trust takes time. That isn't always true. Trust is a formula and a process that usually takes time to play out. When we follow these steps and authentically check these boxes, trust happens faster. When we are intentional and move away from a lateral or superficial line of questioning into a much deeper one, people feel listened to and heard.

Sometimes People Suck

Even with the LOVE method to conversation, we sometimes come across people who aren't very nice and are selfish, arrogant, or even mean. When we find those people, that's OK. We simply end the conversation and move on. In a sales environment, that's a good thing because no one really wants to do business with someone who doesn't share the same values. They will make life hard and refer others who are like them to you.

However, because we weren't trying to get something from them in return, we were authentically trying to find something we liked about them. And if they were mean, we don't feel rejected. We just move on and count our blessings that we dodged a bullet.

None of this is easy. It takes discipline to listen to others rather than talk about ourselves. It takes self-awareness, and it takes intentional effort.

The LOVE Game

It's game time again. A great way to implement this skill in your everyday toolkit is to play the LOVE game. After all, perfect practice makes perfect.

With the LOVE game, we get together as a group of two or more people to test our skills at LOVE. Put one person in the hot seat and have them start with a conversation opener. The next person must *listen, observe, validate,* and *expand.* Based on the answer, the following person must then *listen, observe, validate,* and *expand.* And the process repeats.

There is a catch, however. When someone misses the sequence, doesn't validate, or starts a new thread of conversation that wasn't built on what was said previously, the game starts over.

Don't be fooled. It's not an easy game. Most groups at first take 15–20 minutes to get past the first three people.

As stress increases, it's harder to listen and more mistakes happen. It is critical that you don't go easy on the steps. The stress of accountability is paramount. This is by design and is an essential part of the exercise.

Once the group gets into a groove and realizes they don't want to keep starting over, they focus, lean in, cut out all distractions, and magically, they get around the circle easily. Listening is an active sport that requires an empty mind with no agenda.

This exercise is great for teams and even family dinners to teach kids the skill of conversation and connection. They may hate it at first but will come back and thank you later when they lean on this skill to survive the realities life throws at them.

Speaking from the Heart

Well-chosen language, spoken in the right manner and with congruent body language, can touch the heart and soul, find common ground, tear down walls of division, foster powerful new relationships, and move people to action. Language that ignores another person's emotional state, culture, current life situation, and personal beliefs misses its mark. Instead of building trust, it can distance us from those we care about and those we need to influence.

You have the answers, capability, and tools to be an outstanding communicator. In fact, you've had them all along, and the best part, they're all free. Good eye contact, active listening, and being sensitive to others' stress levels and backgrounds are all things you know to be important.

Perhaps they have become so familiar we may have lost sight of their value and subsequently stopped using them. Now is the time to remind yourself of the importance of these fundamentals and to apply them. Doing so will make the difference between winning and losing a sale, landing the job and not getting a call back, or getting through to your children about the importance of saying no to drugs versus having the kids ignore you.

I hope this message helps you become a bit paranoid about your communication—paranoid enough to slow down, think before you speak, and listen before you respond.

Don't give up. Keep practicing, and sooner rather than later you will master the lost art of conversation.

Powerful Takeaways

- Communication is tough, especially when we are under stress.
- No matter how good a communicator we think we are, the reality is we are ineffective at communication.
- Interpersonal communication has filters; your personal filter is the way you see, engage with, and understand the world around you and inside you.
- A considerable degree of miscommunication is caused by misinterpreting the intended needs of people.
- People want to feel that they have been heard. That can only be determined by them, not us.
- The best leaders, managers, parents, sales professionals, and conversationalists do the same thing in conversation. They LOVE—an acronym for listen, observe, validate, and expand.
- Bombarding people with lots of information in the hopes that some of it may get them to like us more results in a boring, one-sided conversation that never amounts to anything. When that happens in any persuasive or influence scenario, people notice it, raise their natural resistance, and make connection even more difficult.
- Well-chosen language, spoken in the right manner and with congruent body language, can touch the heart and soul, find common ground, tear down walls of division, foster powerful new relationships, and move people to action.

12

The Stress Factor

"Stress can sabotage our ability to influence."

—René Rodriguez

ALL THE METHODS, techniques, sequences, scripts, and values in this book don't matter if you can't access them when you are stressed. Let that sink in for a minute.

Part of Our Daily Lives

It is easy to lead when times are good. It is easy to get people to agree if they already agree with you. But to spark an idea in the mind of the opposition, to have the emotional discipline to not react in the face of hostility, and to find your best strategic response requires advanced skills that are rooted in understanding the role stress plays in our lives day-to-day.

Even after thousands of speeches, the best speakers will admit to being nervous before presentations. That's OK. Nerves are the mind and body's way of letting us know something is important.

But stress hinders your ability to perform at your best and therefore sabotages your ability to influence. Top sports performers, speakers, and sales professionals all learn to manage their stress so it doesn't interfere with their performance. Personally, after thousands of presentations, I still feel the nerves, pressure, and stress of performing at my best. The difference now is that I have learned not only to manage the stress but also to use it to focus. I learned a long time ago that the nerves will never go away, and you really don't want them to.

> *"It's all right to have butterflies in your stomach. Just get them to fly in formation."*
> *—Robert Gilbert, PhD, professor of sports psychology, Montclair State University, motivation expert and author.*[1]

Elite performers—from professional athletes to Navy SEALS, and CEOs who run massive organizations—are under incredible pressure to perform. If they don't, the consequences can be extreme. At the elite level, it's no longer about knowhow. That's because everyone basically has the same strengths, the same speed, the same level of experience, and they know the ins and outs of their expertise. What really sets the elite apart is their ability to perform under stress, period.

Understanding the Science

One way to learn to control stress is to understand the science behind it and why sometimes we can't totally control it.

Let's start with understanding that there are two systems or minds in our brain that dictate our behavior. Psychologists Keith Stanovich and Richard West coined them as systems 1 and 2.[2] This theory was made popular by psychologist and Nobel Laureate Daniel Kahneman, who is also the founding father of modern behavioral economics. His groundbreaking work illustrated in his book *Thinking Fast and Slow* points out that most of our responses to life can be categorized by these two systems.

System 1: Fast Thinking

This type of thinking is powered by the autonomic nervous system and is automatic. Remember sequence, the brain, and how it triggers our fight/flight/freeze responses? The amygdala is our panic button. The thalamus is the brain's relay station. And the hypothalamus connects to the autonomic nervous system, which controls the parasympathetic or calm response and the sympathetic or excited-response nervous systems. These are automatic responses, the aspects of life that we don't have to think about: breathing, heartbeat, digestion, walking, simple math, etc.

Think of a picture of a person who is furious at someone else. Perhaps their fists are up, face flushed, and they are in mid-scream. Looking at the picture, we can't actually hear the scream or what they're saying, but we can imagine it, and we definitely know the person is angry. All this happens effortlessly and automatically, behind the scenes without us ever realizing it's happening. We don't come to that conclusion over time; we do it instantaneously. That's referred to as fast thinking. One might even call this system more primitive.

Some examples of how system 1 works automatically include:

- Detecting whether an object is near or far away;
- The ability to orient ourselves to sound in a room;
- Finishing a cliché, such as "bread and . . .";
- Involuntarily making a face of disgust when you see something horrible;
- Detecting hostility in a voice;
- Driving home on an empty, familiar road;
- Walking at a normal pace;
- Solving the simple equation $2 + 2 = ?$

These are automatic responses that don't require much of our brain's energy.

System 2: Slow Thinking

Now look at the following equation: $17 \times 485 = x$. We immediately know this is a mathematical problem, and most of us need a piece of paper and a pencil or a calculator to solve it. But we are the only species that can solve the equation.

Those of us who are mathematically inclined may automatically know a possible range of outcomes, too—that the total is more than a certain number and less than another. Whether we're math geniuses or not, though, most of us recognize all this quickly without slowing down or spending time with the problem. Realistically, we don't know the solution instantly because the precise answer doesn't come to mind immediately and requires more attention and energy. This is what's known as slow thinking.

The process of slow thinking requires us to recall certain events or, in this instance, lessons learned in school. Then we draw conclusions—solve the problem. Slow thinking is not automatic. System 2 allocates our attention to the more difficult mental activities, including complex computations, and is typically associated with the subjective experiences of choice and concentration. When we feel like we're in control, that's a system 2 experience.

Here are several examples of system 2, which require real brain energy:

- Focusing on finding a specific person in a crowd;
- Mentally preparing yourself for a big event—a race perhaps or even a presentation;
- Trying to recall a familiar song on the radio;

- Walking fast to keep up with someone else;
- Managing your behavior in a social setting;
- Comparing or contrasting the value of similar items;
- Identifying a pattern on a page;
- Assessing the validity of an argument.

These are system 2 functions, which require time and focus and are uniquely human.

System 2 Is at the Mercy of System 1

Every day these two systems battle to be in control. System 1 takes the short-term perspective on what matters at the moment. That means if you have a goal that requires sacrifice and delay of gratification, then system 1 can work against you.

At the same time, system 2 is trying to remind you of why you're trying to accomplish the goal. We can think of system 1 as like a superhero. Its job is to protect you from evil—in this instance, stress.

Compare and contrast. Procrastination is a great way to explain these differences. Let's say you're getting ready for a presentation to 1,000 people. The thought of walking out in front of that huge audience starts to trigger stress.

Stress can be deadly, so as protection your system 1 kicks in and says, "There's a problem. The perfect solution is to put the project off and do it tomorrow."

So you put off the project, and system 1 did its job. You're no longer stressed.

At the same time, system 2 tells you that you're an idiot to procrastinate. Don't put the project off. But system 1 is in control, and everything seems like smooth sailing.

The same scenario happens repeatedly, and you keep delaying the project. But if you keep listening to system 1, at some point the tables turn and the stress moves from being caused by fear of doing the project to not having it completed and facing the consequences.

System 1 Is Only Short Term

At that point, system 1 shows up again because you're still stressed. It says, "No problem. The perfect solution is stay up all night and get the project done." System 1 has shifted protecting you from the stress of starting to the stress of the consequences of not finishing.

That's a lot to think about. Our lives—personal and professional—are a constant battle between systems 1 and 2. No wonder we're stressed!

But when we understand the basic relationship and the workings of these two opposing systems, we can begin to master them.

The job of system 1 is to protect us from stress and of system 2 to prepare us for the longer term. That applies to everything from talking to an audience of one or 1,000 to setting financial goals, reluctance to make sales calls, creating healthy eating habits, and so much more.

System 1 and Speaking

When we are about to speak, make a pitch, or enter an important influence scenario, the likelihood of system 1 entering the picture is high. Thus, the ability and skill to master your stress levels are paramount to becoming an effective influencer and leader. All the preparation and study in the world won't alleviate that stress if we can't learn to manage our system 1. Each of us needs to learn the tools to help us handle system 1 and then practice, practice, practice.

Apply the Learning: Stress Reducer

Nerves are normal. The key is to learn how to ease the stress. Watch how this simple ice breaker changes the energy of the room. Before your next presentation/talk/ speech, try this:

- *As soon as you take the stage, address your audience: "Before we get started, I'd like to ask everyone to stand up. If you are like most people today, you are bombarded with information and requests for your time and energy. The fact that you are here is a huge honor for me and for (your host's name), so we want to thank you for that. If you would, I'd like you to just take a moment and shake three people's hands. You only have 30 seconds, so stay focused. Go!"*
- *After about one minute, ask the audience to take their seats. You will immediately notice the entire room has a higher energy level, people will be smiling, and their body posture will be more relaxed and taking up more space. The audience is energized and engaged.*

Box Breathing

Since stress is a physiological response, you can use physical approaches to calm it. An effective way to focus energy and manage stress is box breathing. Also known as square breathing, this technique is widely used by US Navy SEALS and works to calm nerves. You can even download box-breathing apps to your smart phone. (Check a few out on the App Store on your phone.)

The breathing technique calls for a person to inhale for 4 seconds, hold for 4 seconds, exhale for 4 seconds and hold for 4 seconds. It's 4-4-4-4. That process and structure trigger a parasympathetic nervous system response, which is the relaxed response, as opposed to the sympathetic, or excitatory, nervous system, which controls the stress response. Those two systems are antagonistic—they can't function at the same time.

This process takes practice, and the numbers matter. When you can follow the 4-4-4-4 pattern, your entire body begins to move into system 2 allowing you to be more intentional about your responses. This is a great technique when you feel stress rising in the middle of a presentation or just before going on stage. The more you practice this, the easier it becomes, and over time you will learn to almost breath naturally this way without anyone knowing it.

3-in, 4-out Method

I use another similar and simpler method that I learned from the Mayo Clinic. It is simply three seconds in and four seconds out. It is important to get that fourth second to trigger the relaxed response. If you exhale too fast—you'll feel it—you will begin to hyperventilate, which has the opposite effect on your sympathetic nervous system, triggering more stress.

Over time, you can practice extending the exhale longer and longer to what is most comfortable. My sweet spot is about an eight- to nine-second exhale. Even one good breath with a long exhale can immediately change your state. To prevent exhaling too fast, purse your lips together making it harder for the air to pass through. This gives you more control. You'll be able to better hear the exhale, too, which serves as an auditory feedback loop, which can be calming.

Progressive Relaxation

If you've ever heard stories of Olympic gold medal winners or championship teams using relaxation as a secret to success, most likely they used some form of progressive relaxation developed by US physician Edmund Jacobson (1888–1983). The technique trains you to relax the entire body by building awareness of what muscle group harbors your tension and then relaxing one muscle group at a time. You are guided to consciously tense specific muscles or muscle groups and then release them to achieve relaxation throughout the body.

Progressive relaxation is different and serves a different purpose from box breathing or 3-in/4-out. It is designed to build a connection between mind and body and to help us understand that stress is a physical response.

We have used this for more than 30 years in our courses to help build trust and teamwork with groups as well as with leaders before they give presentations.

Progressive Relaxation

Here is the script for progressive relaxation that we use with our clients:

If you would, sit comfortably, close your eyes, take a deep breath and tell yourself to relax.

- *. . . And take another deep breath and tell yourself to relax and notice how your body does just what you tell it to do. You say,"relax,"and it does.*
- *. . . Another deep breath and very gently tell yourself to relax.*
- *. . . And tense up your toes as tightly as you can. And relax those muscles. And relax those muscles even more.*
- *. . . And as you begin to tense up the muscles in the lower part of your legs, observe the process. Don't just do it. Observe the process your muscles go through. Observe*

(Continued)

the process as you relax those muscles and tell those muscles to relax even more.

■ . . . Observing the process, tense up the muscles in the upper part of your legs. This is what your body feels like when it's in a state of tension. Were you aware of it, or is this new information for you? And relax those muscles. And communicate to those muscles to relax even more.

■ . . . And tense up the muscles in your abdomen and lower back and, as you do, notice how much pressure you're putting on the organs in that part of your body. And yet, quite often when we hear bad news, we physically tense up. And relax those muscles. And relax them even more.

■ . . . And tense up the muscles in the upper part of your torso. Hunch up your shoulders, tense the muscles in your upper back and chest and smoothly and gently relax those muscles. And relax them even more.

■ . . . And tense up the muscles in both arms by clenching both fists. Make tense, taut fists. As you do, notice how much physical vitality it takes to keep your muscles this tense, the drain on your physical energy. Be aware of it and relax those muscles. And communicate to those muscles to relax even more.

■ . . . And tense up every muscle in your face that you can, particularly around the eyes and the jaw, two areas where many of us carry a lot of stress, and relax those muscles. And relax them even more.

■ . . . And let your head come forward and very slowly and very, very gently begin to rotate your head in a big, wide circle, first in one direction and then in the other, very slowly, very gently, not forcing it, to relax the muscles in your neck and your upper shoulder area, another place many people carry a lot of stress.

- ■ *. . . And tense up every muscle in your body beginning at your toes, working up your legs through your abdomen and back, clench your fists, and make a tense, taut face.*
- ■ *. . . Very slowly, as if you were moving in slow motion, relax every muscle in your body. Very slowly, very smoothly and very, very gently relax every muscle in your body and tell those muscles to let go and communicate to every cell and every muscle of your entire body to relax even more.*
- ■ *. . . And take your mind or your imagination to the top of your head and take your mind or your imagination on a trip down through your physical body. When it comes to a muscle that's not relaxed, tense up that muscle even more, hold it to the count of three, four, five, six, whatever is comfortable for you and relax it. Do that as many times to as many muscles as necessary to release the stress from your physical body.*
- ■ *. . . And take a deep breath and open your eyes, maintaining that very relaxed state of mind and body.*

Source: ENGAGE™

If you practice this only three times, you will begin to notice exactly where you physically keep your stress. Though people teach progressive relaxation as a skill to relax your entire body, a quick way to release stress before a meeting is to take a moment to be mindful, figure out where your body holds stress—identify what muscle(s) are holding the stress and then tense that muscle, hold it, and then release it. You will immediately feel the calm over your entire body if you go through the full process.

With a little practice, you'll see massive results immediately. But, again, it takes consistent practice to master.

More Tips to Manage Stress

In addition to box breathing, when you don't have time to take a nap, run a mile, or take a yoga class, here are a few quick tips on how to reduce stress levels:

* Listen to music; often, classical music can be very relaxing.
* Take a quick walk, even around the block.
* Find the sun, seriously; bright light can be a quick pick-me-up.
* Count backward; try 1–10 and then 10–1.
* Alone time; take 5 minutes to collect your thoughts and clear your head.
* Eat chocolate; dark chocolate can regulate levels of cortisol, the stress hormone.
* Meditate; five minutes is all it takes.
* Chew gum; it lowers cortisol levels.
* Try green tea; it has calming chemicals including L-theanine.
* Laugh; science has shown it can ease tension.
* Drip cold water on your wrists; try a few drops on your wrists and ear lobes.
* Try some honey; science backs this up, too.

Source: https://www.ncbi.nlm.nih.gov/pmc/articles/PMC1375238/?tool=pubmed; https://www.ncbi.nlm.nih.gov/pmc/articles/PMC4020454/; https://www.colorado.edu/law/25-quick-ways-reduce-stress

Powerful Takeaways

- Two systems in our brain control our actions. When we understand the basic relationship and the workings of these two opposing systems, we can begin to master them.
- Even the best speakers will admit to being nervous before presentations. That's OK. Nerves are the mind and body's way of letting us know something is important.
- The ability and skill to master your stress levels are paramount when it comes to being an effective influencer and leader.
- Progressive relaxation builds a connection between mind and body and helps us understand that stress is a physical response.

13

Putting It All Together and More

"With the rewards of influence also come responsibilities."
—*René Rodriguez*

IN ALL THE years of doing this work, seeing everything *click* for someone is among my favorite moments. It's true joy to watch someone who has struggled to communicate their message embark on the journey to uncover their own story and discover the discipline to learn the skills to communicate effectively.

When all that comes together, I see someone's life change in an instant. The clarity of focus they find is inspiring. The effortless way they tell their story and transition to powerful and relevant tie-downs is like watching a gymnast nail a perfect 10 landing at the Olympics. People also begin to see themselves differently. They stand taller, speak louder, and take bolder steps.

We began this journey talking about the opposite of influence—when no one laughs at our jokes, buys our products, or follows our visions. When that happens, people feel sad, lonely, and insignificant. To watch someone instead find their significant place in the world and connect it to their purpose and values is unforgettable. It's also a deliberate process that can be replicated over and over.

225

Having confidence and knowing that you can communicate any message so people will not only listen to but also act on it is energizing. Having the self-awareness to know when people resist and the skills to overcome that resistance to deliver a message opens doors to opportunities. The ability to influence in areas where others can't truly has a powerful effect on the world. To spark an idea in the opposition—"I never thought about it like that before," for example—is the kind of influence we need in today's world.

Delayed Flight

I was leaving Columbus, Oklahoma, and heading to an event that started the next morning. At 8 a.m., 50 executives would be sitting in a room expecting me to lead a workshop. But my flight was delayed—and not only my flight but also many others. When I heard that news, I could feel my stress level rise—a system 1 reaction.

Predictable

What happened next was predictable. The line in front of the airport gate agent, who was trying to rebook people, began to grow. The longer the wait lasted, the more riled those in line became. People started to get out of line and approach the counter waving their tickets and demanding that they be rebooked.

The gate agent was a total pro. Cool, calm, and collected, she told the agitated travelers, "Yelling at me isn't going to make this go any faster."

The controlled chaos continued for almost an hour until the agent announced that all flights were booked and she was working on finding other seats for passengers.

I decided to sit back and watch as people yelled at her. All I could think about was how frustrating her position must be.

So I walked around to the side of the counter and said, "Excuse me, I'm going to get a coffee. What do you drink? I'll get you one. It's going to be a long night." She looked at me, dropped her shoulders and said, "Oh my goodness, are you serious? I would kill for a grande caramel macchiato . . . You are too sweet."

I returned, placed the drink on her counter, and walked away. Before I could sit down, though, she said "Hey, stay in my line of sight." I nodded and sat down. About 25 minutes later, she waved me over, handed me a ticket, and said, "Enjoy your flight, Mr. Rodriguez."

A Closer Look

Let's break this down. You could make the case that I didn't use any framing, deliver any profound message, or do anything more than buy her a coffee and yet got what I wanted. The truth is, I don't know if I received special treatment or if everyone was rebooked on a flight at that point.

What I do know is that I didn't succumb to my first reaction, which was to go into system 1 like everyone else. Despite the stress, I didn't yell, wave my ticket, or demand I get a new flight. The discipline and self-awareness—not reacting—in that particular moment is a huge part of influence and will serve you better in the long run than hysteria.

While everyone was up in arms (system 1), I sat back and watched what unfolded. That enabled me to empathize with the ticket agent. That empathy allowed me to connect through an act of kindness in a moment of need. I didn't have any expectation that I would get anything for my gesture, I just did it.

Did part of me understand that a gesture like that immediately made me stand out from others? Absolutely. My desire to stand out by serving someone in their time of need is no different from any salesperson, recruiter, leader, or the people yelling at her in line. They wanted to stand out and chose yelling as their tool. I chose patience, empathy, and coffee. Had I not had discipline, self-awareness, empathy, emotional intelligence, and assertiveness, I wouldn't have had the chance to stand out.

Sometimes influence is setting yourself up in the best strategic position possible. Then you control what you can control and nothing more. It doesn't work every time. But does it work more than the person who doesn't try it? Absolutely! There are no silver bullets, so don't look for them. What you want is an accumulation of subtle advantages that accrue over time. A racehorse only needs to win by a nose. The same works with influence, too.

Ethical Influence

The world of influence can be very rewarding and with those rewards comes a lot of responsibility. Just because you can influence or convince someone of something, does not mean you should.

That's where the ethical conversation comes into play. I urge you to spend some time with the ethical dilemma because it forces you to think beyond yourself and into how what you do affects others.

Impact: To be an effective leader, you must have the ability to influence. Remember the definition: *To influence is to have an impact on the behaviors, attitudes, opinions, and choices of others.*

Influence versus Manipulation

Some say that influence is another way to manipulate people. I spent many years studying and researching the difference between manipulation and influence because it is a very fair question that should be asked.

The reality is that everyone uses influence to get what they want whether they are trained influencers or not. People learn at a young age that certain sequences, looks, patterns, and phrases work better than others. That's part of the human experience. Children sometimes learn that crying and tantrums get them what they want. Some adults learn that guilting and shaming get them what they want. Some people bully and push to get what they want; others use flattery and niceties to manipulate. We talked about "nice guys" passively being nice to drive their hidden agenda.

Transparency is key. What sets influence apart from manipulation is that influence most often happens transparently with both parties fully aware of it. There is no need to hide it. Influence isn't power or control; it's about building trust and communicating value.

Impact is the key word. A great story from a pastor can impact your day and decisions to be a better and more honest person. A child's story about cancer can impact you to donate to children's cancer research. These are positive things and use all the principles you've learned in this book.

Extreme. Manipulation has a distinct definition. *Manipulation is using persuasion to an extreme at the expense of another person and is often done without the person's knowledge.* Key words being *extreme* and *expense.* There are plenty of studies about manipulation and countless books that teach people step-by-step how to manipulate people and groups.

It can be a good idea to understand manipulation because its origins are the same as those of influence. Both are rooted in our neurological and biological make up.

Example. At a recent conference, a well-known speaker was negotiating hard for their speaker fee. There's nothing wrong with a good negotiation, but every time both parties reached an agreement, the would-be speaker kept changing it, adding to the contract. The back-and-forth continued. The speaker was betting that once a decision was made to work with them, it would become harder to back out and easier for new agreements to creep in.

The speaker gave an ultimatum that demanded a ridiculous sum even though they had earlier agreed on an amount. The conference owners were fed up, called the speaker out, and passed on the entire relationship. Then, as predicted, the speaker offered to agree to the original terms. The conference team had already lost trust in the speaker and opted not to hire them.

It was an unfortunate and frustrating situation because of the lack of ethics and integrity displayed. I was highly impressed by the conference team for their steadfast commitment to their values even in the face of negotiating with a quasi-celebrity.

This is a classic form of strong-arm manipulation using pressure, momentum, and a bet on people's tendency to be agreeable and avoid conflict. Sadly, that works on many people. That is *not* influence; it is unethical, sleazy manipulation.

Using influence in a situation like this would look very different. For example:

- Writing a book or article to create strong ethos and demand;
- Having a strong presentation that clearly ties someone's keynote to the intended objectives and theme of an event;
- Utilizing a powerful speaker reel and client testimonials to reduce the feeling of risk.

Cost of Not Hiring You

A running joke among my close friends is the way I respond whenever someone asks, "What does it cost to bring you in?" My response is the exact same every time. It utilizes many of the skills and principles you've learned in this book.

Client: "So how much does it cost to bring you in?"

Me: "I'm sorry, to bring me in or not to bring me in?"

With that interchange, I get one of two responses. Either the potential client laughs or giggles and says, "Ha ha; to bring you in. That was good." Or with a somewhat perplexed but intrigued look they slowly say, "To bring you in." Either way my response is typically the same.

Me: "I say that somewhat facetiously because if it costs you more to bring me in than not doing so, it won't cost you anything because you just won't bring me in. It wouldn't make any business sense to use my services. *But* if there is a solution that I can bring to the table that solves a problem for you that far exceeds the cost of bringing me in, would you agree that there would be a cost to not solving that problem?"

The amount of logic used in that response is fair and triggers a real business conversation around what actually matters— value. I have never had anyone disagree with that logic, and the response is typically something along the following:

Client: "That actually makes a lot of sense."

Me: "So what I'd like to do is to learn more about your business, what your goals are, and see where my skill sets and solutions might be able to provide value that far exceeds the cost of bringing me in. My goal is always to offer value at least three to five times greater than my cost. And if I don't do that, I won't charge you anything, and your only risk would be time—something we would both invest together."

Even clients with whom I have worked for years ask me the same question and then immediately follow up with, "Yeah, yeah I know. What does it cost to not bring you in?" And my response to that is always the same, and I say it with a big smile.

Me: "Great, yes, let's talk about the value we are trying to create together."

I use this scenario as an example of an ethical and transparent way to reframe a conversation around what I personally feel and believe to be more important than price, which is value. This example also illustrates the transparent and authentic nature of the methodology. It doesn't have to be sneaky when it comes from an honest place founded on fundamental truths.

Important: To be able to deliver a script like that, you first must believe in this philosophy, which I do to my core. If you struggle with the price objection or with your personal value, then you might have a hard time authentically delivering this script. My suggestion is to put your business hat on and do the math exactly as I suggested. Offer three to five times more value that what you charge for your services. If you can't do that, then you have other problems to solve first.

Influence in Life versus Presentation

Many of the examples above are about using influence in real life situations. Framing and tie-downs apply to all aspects of life, whether in normal day-to-day conversations or well-structured formal presentations.

That's where the AMPLIFII checklist comes in handy.

The AMPLIFII Checklist

Everything you've learned in this book can be summed up in the AMPLIFII checklist. It's a list of questions that can help you *create* a talk or a message and not *deliver* it. There's an important distinction between the two.

These are the steps I follow every time I craft a message, put together a presentation, or give a talk. Let's take a closer look.

1. Who is my audience?
2. What is my influence objective (IO)?
3. What is my value proposition or core message?
4. What frame best sets up my message?
5. Is my ethos (credibility) in good standing?
6. Does my frame trigger the appropriate pathos (emotions)?
7. Does my message make logical (logos) sense?
8. Is my tie-down clear and does my audience understand what my message means to them?
9. Is my message relevant and current (kairos)?
10. Am I clear as to where I am going with my message (telos)?

Each of these steps serves a very important purpose in the influence process. If you think about it, an entire book was written to back up just ten steps to help you create the perfect presentation/talk.

Who Is My Audience?

This is *always* the first and the most important question. Your audience determines everything. If you were speaking to a group of 13-year-olds, your message would be very different from one to a group of referral partners.

This question also helps you get in the right frame of mind to think of the customer/audience first. It isn't about us; it's about them. Always begin with the audience as it will give you the context you need for crafting the entire presentation.

What Is My Influence Objective (IO)?

You need to be clear and simple about this question. Too many people try to get cute and fancy. Think of the next action that needs to be taken to move the company forward. Make it tangible, too. For example, "I want to set up a 30-minute phone call," or "I want them to agree to 8 a.m. September 25."

Stay away from intangible objectives such as "a meet and greet" or "for them to see what we are about." The latter are hard to measure and don't move the process forward.

What Is My Value Proposition or Core Message?

Given that you are trying to influence something, what is valuable to the listener? What information or message needs to be communicated?

Remember the "planting seeds in cement" analogy? This is the seed you want to plant.

What Frame Best Sets Up the Message?

I've discussed many different framing devices. Stories are the most powerful, with your origin story at the top of the list. But jokes, statistics, props, and even magic tricks (if you are any good) can be great.

It all comes down to what you want to accomplish. Or if we go back to the golf bag analogy, what part of the course are you on and what club is best for the circumstances.

Is My Ethos in Good Standing?

This is one of the most important questions to ask and includes multiple layers. First, this is a preemptive strategy in which you take inventory of the situation up front to avoid any surprises.

It's an ideal situation to use the 3Ps tool—predict, preempt, prevent. This is also where it's important to determine if there is any threat to your credibility—ethos—before making your presentation.

If a threat is present, then employ preemptive measures to remedy that threat before it sabotages your influence objective. For example, let's say you are preparing to present a plan to a team, but there are two influential individuals on the team who may not be on board with your plan. If they decide to go against you, it could sway the team.

Most people don't take the time to consider their ethos. And if they do, rather than take preemptive measures, they roll the dice and prepare to go toe-to-toe with any opponents in the meeting—not a smart move. Here is a better strategy.

Set up a meeting with each person individually and take the following approach:

> *John, I wanted to connect before the budget meeting and make sure you and I are on the same page. You are such a critical member of this team, and if for some reason you didn't agree with my plan, I'd prefer to hash it out before the meeting so we could align. Besides, you may have some insights that I may have missed.*

Being transparent about your intentions and desire for alignment is ethical and a mark of respect for your colleague.

A similar situation can be one in which you don't have any opposing threats in the meeting but you do need the team to wake up and take action. You may want to have some pre-meeting individual discussions with the more influential people and enroll them as advocates before the main meeting. Whereas in the past these people have been quiet and passively supportive, ask for their leadership and vocal support in the upcoming meeting.

I don't think people ask enough for the support they need. Often, most people don't even realize that others need their support. When you ask for their support, they feel empowered and valued because you gave them a platform for influence, which is always a positive experience.

Other more extreme examples of a threat to your ethos would include if your reputation was muddied in some way—perhaps some legal troubles, a poor previous presentation, a lost temper with a coworker, or even a false rumor.

It is important to note that this isn't about worrying what others think of you. This is about your personal brand and your credibility. You must protect it, so be honest with yourself. If your ethos is at risk, face it and fix it head on with integrity.

Does My Frame Trigger Appropriate Pathos?

Remember, pathos drives people to act on what you are saying. It triggers the emotion and engages them more deeply with you.

Pathos typically is where my clients back out at the last minute. They see the audience and revert to more traditional, logos-heavy presentation styles.

It's tricky because pathos is designed to remind you to allow yourself to deliver the message with emotion and passion. But you also need someone to assess if your presentation actually triggers the appropriate pathos. In the absence of someone to audit your presentation, record it and study it thoroughly and honestly.

Does My Message Make Logical (Logos) Sense?

We have focused on ethos and pathos, but logos is incredibly important, too. Most business professionals gravitate toward logic because there is little vulnerability associated with it.

However, new entrepreneurs often lack logos because they are so passionate (pathos) about their ideas and are frustrated when forced to develop a business plan. To ease the frustration, make sure there is a clear plan of action if needed. Keep it simple to remove any friction or limits on your audience's ability to act.

Is My Tie-Down Clear and Do They Understand What My Message Means To Them?

Spend time to ensure that you speak from your audience's point of view. It's essential that the audience understands what the messages mean to them.

Stay focused on what your audience says and make sure to address their stated as well as underlying needs. Be explicit with your tie-down by using entry ramps such as, "The reason I share this with you is . . ." or "What this means to you is . . ." or "Here's how we will save you money . . ."

Using this type of language not only signals to the audience that value is about to be delivered but also helps you focus on delivering a clear message.

Is My Message Relevant and Current (Kairos)?

If your presentation ventures into potentially risky territory for political correctness, it can be beneficial to elicit the help of others.

For example, if you discuss issues involving the opposite sex, diverse races, or underserved demographics, consider getting feedback from those groups or individuals. They often can provide invaluable guidance and insights. It's also a powerful way to bridge conversations. Most people, after all, want to help.

We are experiencing a time of change, growth, and needed progression. When that happens, we sometimes swing the pendulum too far in one direction as things begin to sort themselves out. That is often frustrating for many people. But be patient, kind, open-minded, and willing to learn. The world is getting smaller, and leaders need to learn how to engage and inspire a wider, more diverse range of people. It is a worthy challenge that will only make us all better human beings.

Am I Clear as to Where I Am Going with My Message (Telos)?

If you are clear about your purpose for your presentation, curveballs, tough questions, or even faulty technology won't throw you off.

Be explicit with how you intend to end a talk or presentation. I learned to first write my ending and then design my presentation around that. Whatever you choose to do, make sure you know the ending and what you hope to accomplish up front.

If you ramble and are lost, you've lost sight of telos. Stop rambling, center your body, place your hands in the influence zone (between belly button and eyes), and say with conviction, "The reason I share this with you is . . ."

Moving directly to the tie-down pulls you immediately back on track and realigns your telos.

Remember, this checklist is not about order of delivery; it's about order of creation. All the steps are critical. And once you get in the habit of following these steps, your brain will automatically start thinking this way.

Practice, Practice, Practice

If you have ever had the privilege of watching a professional athlete train, it is something that sticks with you forever. You will never forget it because of one distinguishing factor: *intensity*. Every move is executed with purpose and intensity. Every fundamental is practiced over and over again to exhaustion to create muscle memory that takes over when the brain shuts off. Every scenario is rehearsed and run through from all angles to prepare them for game time. The goal is that practice should be 10 times harder than a game will ever be.

Professional fighters and Navy SEALs take the same approach—intensity in practice to replicate the intensity of battle. Then, when they go into battle, it isn't their first time. They've been there before, they've sweated this profusely, they've cried these tears, and they've tasted this blood. That is the mentality of greatness.

I know not everyone gravitates to that level of intensity, and it can be easily argued that an amazing life is possible without it. But we are designed to push ourselves to our fullest potential, and we are happiest when we realize our fullest selves and when we have the greatest impact.

The skills shared in this book will require you to put in the time to master them. You will need to fail at them and fail often. You will need to make mistakes and sometimes even bomb in front of a room. It's part of the game. Embrace it and learn everything you can from it. Remember, if you are failing, bombing, and making mistakes, that means you are in the game! You are in the arena of life and not in the stands as a bystander.

Mamba Mentality

The late basketball great Kobe Bryant was legendary for his work ethic and his relentless pursuit to improve his performance.[1] He used to watch all of Michael Jordan's signature moves and would practice exactly what Jordan did and then practice it again.

I was never a Bryant fan until after his tragic death in a helicopter crash. Before that, I saw him as an arrogant, cocky, wannabe Michael Jordan. Then the stories about how hard he worked and his mindset began to reframe how I saw him.

Former professional basketball player Chris Bosh told a Bryant story during his hall of fame speech that sealed my respect for Bryant. Bosh wanted to establish himself as a young leader on the team, so his goal was to wake up by sunrise and be the first to breakfast. He set his alarm, got dressed, and made his way down only to find Bryant was already there with ice packs on his knees, drenched in sweat after a workout.

The power of that story to completely change years of dislike and misunderstanding is something that I often think about. I highly recommend you check it out on YouTube.[2] It's not just the story; it's how Bosh tells the story, his pacing, his timing, and how he sets up each element. I love how his humility came through making Bryant the shining star.

But that speech also solidified Bosh as a leader to me and probably everyone else who heard and saw it—ethos, pathos, logos, kairos, and telos all on display and leaving an impact that will last far beyond my lifetime.

It's the same with your presence and your presentations. If you put in the work and practice every day with game time intensity, eventually you will master the skill of influence.

The Final Tie-Down

The reason I share this entire book with you is . . . you now have the tools to completely transform your life and influence those around you. The question is, What will you do with it? Will you set this book down and go back to your life as it was before you read it? Or will you make a decision to make this a part of your everyday routine? The exploration of your own story is not an easy one. The discipline to learn the skills to deliver your message in a way that is congruent with your values is not an easy one either. But I strongly believe that the most difficult task you have in front of you is to have the courage to use these tools to make a difference in the world. It will be difficult because the times it matters most are when no one around you is listening or cooperating. As I mentioned before, it is easy to lead when times are good, but true leadership is revealed in the struggle.

My wish for you is that you find your voice, put in the work, and take the bold steps necessary to positively influence the world. Don't wait for someone to inspire you or the cavalry to come save you. They aren't coming. The reason they aren't coming is because the cavalry is already here. The inspiration is already here. **It's you.** You are here to inspire people in a way that matches your purpose and story. Uncover it, practice it, and live it boldly. Every day. I can't promise you that it will be easy, but I can promise you that it will be worth it, and the world needs it.

Now go and let your heart speak in sequence.

Powerful Takeaways

- The ability to influence in areas where others can't truly has a powerful effect on the world.
- Influence isn't power or control; it's about building trust and communicating value.
- The world of influence can be very rewarding, and with those rewards comes responsibility. Just because you can influence or convince someone of something, does not mean you should. Spend time thinking about the ethical responsibilities that come with influence.
- Follow the AMPLIFII checklist to create a powerful and influential presentation.
- Practice, practice, practice. The skills you have learned in this book aren't always easy, and it takes practice to master them. The returns and the rewards for your efforts will be well worth the time you spend.

Notes

Chapter 1

1. Sam Carr, "How Many Ads Do We See a Day in 2021," PPC Protect, accessed Nov. 11, 2021, https://ppcprotect.com/blog/strategy/how-many-ads-do-we-see-a-day/.
2. Nancy Gibbs, "Emotional Intelligence: The EQ Factor," *Time* magazine, Vol. 46, Oct. 2, 1995, accessed Nov. 22, 2021, http://content.time.com/time/magazine/0,9263,7601951002,00.html.
3. P. Salovey, J.D. Mayer, "Emotional Intelligence," *Imagination, Cognition and Personality*. 1990; 9(3):185–211. doi:10.2190/DUGG-P24E-52WK-6CDG; https://doi.org/10.2190/DUGG-P24E-52WK-6CDG.
4. P. Salovey, J.D. Mayer, "Daniel Goleman's Five Components of Emotional Intelligence," accessed Nov. 24, 2021, https://web.sonoma.edu/users/s/swijtink/teaching/philosophy_101/paper1/goleman.htm.

Chapter 2

1. Presence Group, "Culture Blunders in Advertising," accessed Oct. 10, 2021, https://www.presencegroup.eu/en/blog/cultural-blunders-advertising.

2. HeartMath, "How Stress Affects the Body," https://www.heartmath.com/blog/health-and-wellness/how-stress-affects-the-body/.

Chapter 3

1. The John Maxwell Company, "7 Factors that Influence Influence," July 8, 2013, accessed Oct. 10, 2021, https://www.johnmaxwell.com/blog/7-factors-that-influence-influence/.
2. BrainPOP Educators, "Sequence Learning Objectives," accessed Nov. 22, 2021, https://educators.brainpop.com/teaching-tip/sequence-learning-objectives/.
3. William A. Kahn, "Psychological Conditions of Personal Engagement and Disengagement at Work," *Academy of Management Journal*, Dec 1990; Vol. 33, No. 4; ProQuest, 708, https://pdfcoffee.com/kahn-1990psychological-conditions-of-personal-engagement-and-disengagement-at-work-pdf-free.html.

Chapter 4

1. Korn Ferry, "A Better Return on Self-Awareness," accessed Nov. 23, 2021, https://www.kornferry.com/insights/briefings-magazine/issue-17/better-return-self-awareness.
2. BusinessWire, "Women Poised to Effectively Lead in Matrix Work Environments, Hay Group Research Finds," March 27, 2012, accessed Nov. 23, 2021, https://www.businesswire.com/news/home/20120327005180/en.
3. Tasha Eurich, "Increase Your Self-Awareness with One Simple Fix," TEDx MileHigh, Dec. 19, 2017, accessed Oct. 20, 2021, https://www.youtube.com/watch?v=tGdsOXZpyWE.
4. Tasha Eurich, "What Self-Awareness Really Is (And How to Cultivate It)", *Harvard Business Review*, Jan. 4, 2018, accessed Oct. 20,2021, https://hbr.org/2018/01/what-self-awareness-really-is-and-how-to-cultivate-it.

5. *Ibid.*
6. *Ibid.*
7. Tasha Eurich, "Increase Your Self-Awareness with One Simple Fix," TEDx MileHigh, Dec. 19, 2017, accessed Oct. 20, 2021, https://www.youtube.com/watch?v=tGdsOXZpyWE.
8. J. Kruger, D. Dunning, "Unskilled and Unaware of It: How Difficulties in Recognizing One's Own Incompetence Lead to Inflated Self-Assessments," *J Pers Soc Psychology*, Dec. 1999, No. 77(6), 1121–34, doi: 10.1037//0022-3514.77.6.1121. PMID: 10626367, https://pubmed.ncbi.nlm.nih.gov/10626367/.

Chapter 6

1. Alan Shepard, "Alan Shepard, 1923–98," Oxford Reference, accessed Oct. 20, 2021, https://www.oxfordreference.com/view/10.1093/acref/9780191826719.001.0001/q-oro-ed4-00016759.
2. The Children's Museum of Indianapolis, "May 5, 1961 Astronaut Alan Bartlett Shepard Jr. Becomes the First American in Space," This Week in History, accessed Oct. 20, 2021, https://www.facebook.com/childrensmuseum/photos/its-nationalastronautdayon-this-day-57-years-ago-astronaut-alan-bartlett-shepard/10156512543708701/.

Chapter 7

1. Mitel Networks, "Businesses Lose an Average of $11,000 per Employee Every Year Due to Ineffective Communications and Collaboration," Globe News Wire, March 23, 2017, accessed Oct. 20, 2021, https://www.globenewswire.com/news-release/2017/03/23/943480/0/en/Businesses-Lose-an-Average-of-11-000-per-Employee-Every-Year-Due-to-Ineffective-Communications-and-Collaboration.html.

2. Dynamic Signal, "Dynamic Signal Study Finds U.S. Workforce Stressed and Ready to Quit, Compounding Concerns From Tight Labor Market and Possible Economic Downturn," GlobeNewswire, March 20, 2019, accessed Oct. 20, 2021, https:// www.globenewswire.com/news-release/2019/03/20/1757785/0/ en/Dynamic-Signal-Study-Finds-U-S-Workforce-Stressed- and-Ready-to-Quit-Compounding-Concerns-From-Tight- Labor-Market-and-Possible-Economic-Downturn.html.

3. Patti van Eys, Dustin Keller, "A 2021 Report on Employee Mental Health," Pathways at Work, accessed Oct. 21, 2021, https://www.pathways.com/pathways-at-work/resources/ employee-mental-health-report. Companies end up paying the price of that stress.

4. Patti van Eys, "HR's Guide to the Effect of Job Stress on Employee Performance," *Pathways*, Sept. 30, 2021, accessed Oct. 21, 2021, https://www.pathways.com/pathways-at-work/ blog/job-stress-and-employee-performance.

5. M.W. Pennington, S.M. Cohen, "Michael E. Porter Speaks on Strategy," *Planning Review*, Vol. 10 No. 1, 8–39, https://doi .org/10.1108/eb053971.

Chapter 8

1. University of California San Francisco Weill Institute for Neurosciences, "Speech & Language," accessed Nov. 1, 2021, https://memory.ucsf.edu/symptoms/speech-language.

2. National Association of Realtors, https://www.nar.realtor/ research-and-statistics/research-reports/highlights-from-the- profile-of-home-buyers-and-sellers.

3. Statscounter, Global Stats, "Desktop vs Mobile vs. Tablet Worldwide http Market Share Guam, Oct. 2020–Oct. 2021," accessed Nov. 1, 2021, https://gs.statcounter.com/platform- market-share/desktop-mobile-tabletWorldwidehttp:/guam/ platform-market-share.

4. Startup Info Team, "7 Powerful Marketing Statistics for 2021," Startup Info.com, May 24, 2021, https://startup.info/7-powerful-video-marketing-statistics-for-2021/.

5. National Association of Realtors, "Highlights from the Profile of Buyers and Sellers," Research and Statistics, Research Reports, https://www.nar.realtor/research-and-statistics/research-reports/highlights-from-the-profile-of-home-buyers-and-sellers.

6. Statscounter, Global Stats, "Desktop vs. Mobile vs. Market Share Worldwide," accessed Nov. 1, 2021, https://gs.statcounter.com/platform-market-share/desktop-mobile-tabletWorldwidehttp:/guam/platform-market-share.

7. Startup Info Team, "7 Powerful Marketing Statistics for 2021," Startup Info.com, May 24, 2021, https://startup.info/7-powerful-video-marketing-statistics-for-2021/.

8. Jordan Wittmeyer, "Roundabouts vs. Intersections: It's time to revolutionize the ways in which we travel," Hamburg High School, Jan. 14, 2020, accessed Nov. 1, 2021, https://storymaps.arcgis.com/stories/a8c16fc4646e443e9b26a5c641b6fbcd.

Chapter 9

1. Lauren Cook, AMNY, "A Brief History of Blackouts in New York City," July 15, 2019, https://www.amny.com/news/blackouts-nyc-1-33881190/.

2. Jim Rohn, *The Art of Exceptional Living*, Simon & Schuster, accessed Nov. 1, 2021, https://www.goodreads.com/quotes/757767-there-are-some-things-you-don-t-have-to-know-how.

3. Kalina Christoff, Alan M. Gordon, Jonathan Smallwood, Rachelle Smith, Jonathan W. Schooler, "Experience Sampling During fMRI Reveals Default Network and Executive System Contributions to Mind Wandering," *PNAS*, May 26, 2009, 106(21) 8719–8724, accessed Nov. 1, 2021, https://doi.org/10.1073/pnas.0900234106.

4. Kris Snibbe, "Wandering Mind Not a Happy Mind," *The Harvard Gazette*, July 15, 2019, accessed Nov. 15, 2021, https://news.harvard.edu/gazette/story/2010/11/wandering-mind-not-a-happy-mind/.

5. St. Louis Community College Libraries, "Classical Mythology—Greek," *Research Guides*, accessed Nov. 10, 2021, https://guides.stlcc.edu/c.php?g=154584&p=1015055.

6. Parkinson's NSW, "Four Happy Hormones," accessed Nov. 1, 2021, https://www.parkinsonsnsw.org.au/four-happy-hormones.

7. Lani Peterson, "The Science Behind the Art of Storytelling," *Harvard Business Publishing*, Nov. 14, 2017, accessed Nov. 10, 2021, https://www.harvardbusiness.org/the-science-behind-the-art-of-storytelling/.

8. Paul J. Zak, "Why Your Brain Loves Good Storytelling," *Harvard Business Review*, Oct. 28, 2014, accessed Nov. 1, 2021, https://hbr.org/2014/10/why-your-brain-loves-good-storytelling.

9. *Ibid.*

10. Alan S. Brown, Kathryn Croft Caderao, Lindy M. Fields, Elizabeth J. Marsh, "Borrowing Personal Memories," *Applied Cognitive Psychology*, May/June 2015, Vol. 29, 3, 471–477, https://doi.org/10.1002/acp.3130, accessed Nov. 1, 2021, https://onlinelibrary.wiley.com/doi/10.1002/acp.3130.

Chapter 10

1. University of Wisconsin-Extension, "Taking Care of You: Body, Mind, and Spirit," accessed Oct. 10, 2021, https://fyi.extension.wisc.edu/takingcareofyou/files/2018/09/3-hr-TCY-General-Overview.pdf.

2. Daniel Goleman, *Emotional Intelligence: Why It Can Matter More than IQ*, accessed Oct. 10, 2021, https://www.danielgoleman.info/.

3. Taylor Dury, Keith McGowan, Danika Kramer, Cassie Lovejoy, "First Impressions: The Factors of Influence," ResearchGate, Jan. 2009, accessed Nov. 10, 2021, https://www.researchgate

.net/publication/241796494_First_Impressions_The_Factors_of_Influence.

4. University of Glasgow, "First Impressions Count, New Speech Research Confirms," Medical Press, Oct. 22, 2018, accessed Nov. 21, 2021, https://medicalxpress.com/news/2018-10-speech.html.

5. Jon Michail, "Strong Nonverbal Skills Matter Now More than Ever in this New Normal," Forbes Coaches Council, Aug. 24, 2020, accessed Nov. 10, 2021, https://www.forbes.com/sites/forbescoachescouncil/2020/08/24/strong-nonverbal-skills-matter-now-more-than-ever-in-this-new-normal/?sh=2bfd677c5c61.

6. Erik Peper, I-Mei Lin, "Increase or Decrease Depression: How Body Postures Influence Your Energy Level," *Biofeedback*, Sept. 1, 2012, 40(3): 125–130, https://doi.org/10.5298/1081-5937-40.3.01.

7. Linda Talley, Samuel Temple, "How Leaders Influence Followers Through the Use of Nonverbal Communication," *Leadership & Organization Development Journal*, Emerald Publishing Limited, March 2, 2015, https://www.emerald.com/insight/content/doi/10.1108/LODJ-07-2013-0107/full/html.

Chapter 11

1. George Bernard Shaw, "Book Browse Favorite Quotes," Book Browse, accessed Nov. 10, 2021, https://www.bookbrowse.com/quotes/detail/index.cfm/quote_number/445/the-single-biggest-problem-in-communication-is-the-illusion-that-it-has-taken-place.

2. Stanley Kubrick, Jan. 17, 2019, Twitter, accessed Nov. 10, 2021, https://twitter.com/stanleykubrick/status/108595994433393971456.

3. Merriam-Webster, "Communication," accessed Nov. 24, 2021, https://www.merriam-webster.com/dictionary/communication.

4. James E. Grunig, Larissa A. Grunig, *The IABC Handbook of Organizational Communication*, 3, accessed Nov. 24, 2021, https://

idr.abu.edu.ng/assets/docs/The%20IABC%20Handbook%20
of%20Organizational%20Communication_%20A%
20Guide%20to%20Internal%20Communication,%20
Public%20Relations,%20Marketing%20and%
20Leadership%20(J-B%20International%20Association%20
of%20Business%20Communicators)%20(%20
PDFDrive%20).pdf#page=35.

Chapter 12

1. Robert Gilbert, Montclair State University, accessed Nov. 1, 2021, http://gilbertsuccesshotline.blogspot.com/.
2. Keith E. Stanovich, Richard F. West, "Individual Differences in Reasoning: Implications for the Rationality Debate?" *Behavioral and Brain Sciences*, 2000, 23, 645–726, accessed Nov. 1, 2021, https://pages.ucsd.edu/~mckenzie/StanovichBBS.pdf.

Chapter 13

1. Kobe Bryant, "The Mind of Kobe Bryant: My Workout, YouTube, Sept. 12, 2019, accessed Oct. 10, 2021, https://www.youtube.com/watch?v=3EHdbuisJzY.
2. Chris Bosh, "Chris Bosh's Basketball Hall of Fame Enshrinement Speech," YouTube, Sept. 11, 2021, accessed Oct. 10, 2021, https://www.youtube.com/watch?v=naCn_91SuVU.

Acknowledgments

"At times, our own light goes out and is rekindled by a spark from another person. Each of us has cause to think with deep gratitude of those who have lighted the flame within us."

—Albert Schweitzer

As I SIT here in a surreal bliss of excitement and exhaustion, I am overcome with gratitude for all the amazing people who have influenced my life. Those who believed in me when I didn't. Those who saw in me what I couldn't. Those who loved me enough to push me beyond what I thought was possible. There are no words that can capture what you mean to me and how much I appreciate you.

Thank you, Mom; you are my inspiration. I hope I've made you proud. This book is a part of your legacy. Thank you, Alex; I am so incredibly proud of you and who you are. You challenge me to be a better person and to live what I believe. I love your tattoo! Thank you, Diego, for these last couple of years for being so independent as all of this came together. Seeing your smile each night gave me the strength to keep pushing even when I was tired. Thank you, Roman, for being a burst of

251

joy everywhere you go. Thank you, Tony Machado, for always including me as one of your children; I'll never forget that.

I want to thank my basketball coaches for never playing me, forcing me to push harder each year, which ironically prepared me for the rejections of life. I want to thank coach Ricky Suggs for being the only coach that "saw me" and telling me, "Keep shooting; a good shooter is either on or he's gonna be on. KEEP SHOOTING!" I'm applying that to life now, coach. I want to thank my favorite professor of all time, Dr. Michael Naughton, for always being willing to talk philosophy with me and pushing me to think harder about ethics, faith, work, and leisure. Those conversations guide me to this day. I want to thank Von Sheppard for all the conversations in his office and the wisdom you imparted that guided me through college. I want to thank Mike Fusek for hiring me into the cookware business at 18 years old right after I got cut from the basketball team. He gave me my first cassette tapes of Zig Ziglar and Jim Rohn and took me to get trained by Tom Hopkins and so many others. You saved me.

I want to thank Dr. Gary Johnson for believing in me and teaching me so much about the brain. If you only knew how much that lighthouse story has influenced my life and thousands of others'. I want to thank Don Klassen for being my first speaking coach and teaching me about influence, tie-downs, and GOSPA. Your impact at such an early age set me on the right track. I want to thank Eric Mitchell always following through on that day at Ciao Bella 17 years ago. Look at us now, brother. I want to thank Tim Braheem for giving me my first big stage at the BP08 Conference in Las Vegas, for Team America, and "the watch." I want to thank Marcelo Montero for mentoring me and guiding me to be a better leader. I cannot express how fortunate I am to have your guidance and experience in my corner. You have made me better even though I fought it at times. I want to thank Ryan Estis for all the coaching, guidance, and generosity in helping me build a speaker business. I hope you see this book and brand as a testimonial to the amazing work you do. I want to thank Seth Mattison for all the collaboration and energy along this journey. Your humility and relentless pursuit of excellence pushes me to keep growing. I want to thank Don and Gino for putting on Momentum Builder during the pandemic, which is how Mike Campbell at Wiley found me. Thanks for seeing the vision, Mike. I want to thank Susan Marks for her tireless work in helping me pulling together a cohesive message from what at times felt like an insurmountable amount of content. I want to thank Mark Madsen for building my first blog and always making time. I want to thank Matt Walsh for his brilliance in helping me quarterback the AMPLIFII brand and for introducing me to Josh. I want to thank Matt Emery and Dennis Warden for pushing me to host a public AMPLIFII event and for coming up with the name AMPLIFII.

The Team

Thank you, **Sam Parker,** for being the first documented transformation. Your video allowed people to understand the power of this process and the incredible human you are.

Thank you, **Dave Savage,** for your friendship and seeing the value in this work. You are such a big part of this story and we aren't done! *fist bump

Thank you, **Elizabeth Hall,** for teaching me what it means to be a leader. For always being in my corner and for pushing me to grow. The plan is working!

Thank you, **Josh Blattermen,** for uncovering my ethos that gave us the words to explain the crazy work I do.

Thank you, **Jorge Castillo,** for your brilliant design and passion for this work. You are such a special human, my friend. I still don't know how you found "neuro" in my name!

Thank you, **Ryan Grams,** for sharing your genius with me and helping us all through this crazy time. You are one of a kind, brother.

Thank you, **Tristan Sagastume,** for capturing so many stories that helped spread the word around this work. You have a bright future, my friend.

Thank you, **Jenny Salimi,** for coming out of the heavens to build this business with me. I can't think of a more perfect person to do what you do. Can you believe how far we've come?

Thank you, **Oscar,** for just being my cousin (brother). You ground me in family. I am so proud of you and who you are.

Thank you, **Jeff, Sandy, Shannon, Parker, Weston, and Aspen,** for accepting me into your family. I can't express how lucky I am to have you all in my life. The love and support you have provided me during this process is hard to explain but has been fully felt. I love you all.

And lastly . . .

Thank you, **Maddy.** I remember sitting at dinner last year as we discussed the idea of writing this book. You forced me to send three emails to publishers I was connected to on LinkedIn while we were on our date. I knew then that you were different, and I loved it. Thank you for taking over when Wiley reached out, to set the timelines, execute the contract, and create a plan for writing this book. Once you took over, there was no looking back as this project was happening. You designed all events and writing time so that we could hit all deadlines. You pushed me relentlessly even though we were in the middle of our busiest time ever. You kept reminding me why we were doing it and how good I would feel after I was done. And here we are.

I could not have done this without you, Maddy. Thank you for pushing me to always be my best. I love you.

About the Author

Born among the palm trees and percussion of Miami, René began splitting his time between Miami and frosty Minnesota as a teen. This continuum of climates and cultures introduced him to the breadth of the human condition at a young age. He then attended the University of St. Thomas, where he began to see the power of applying neuroscience to create personal and professional change.

For over two decades, René has been researching and applying behavioral neuroscience as a dynamic keynote speaker, leadership advisor, world-class sales expert, and renowned speaker coach. He has also trained more than 100,000 people in applying behavioral psychology and neurology methodologies to solve some of the toughest challenges in leadership, sales, and change.

As an entrepreneur and CEO of multiple companies, René integrates a practical business approach that inspires his audiences to take action. Through his keynotes, boot camps, workshops, and proprietary AMPLIFII™ course, he helps us own our backstory to build the frame for our unique and beautiful picture of life.

The result: greater influence, personal transformation, and immediate results in business and life by engaging with courage and grace.

René's engaging speaking style, backed by his scientific approach, makes him a top-rated speaker at every event.

Index